SURVIVAL ARABIC

PHRASEBOOK & DICTIONARY

How to communicate without fuss or fear INSTANTLY!

Revised Edition

by Yamina Gharsa and
Fethi Mansouri

TUTTLE Publishing

Tokyo | Rutland, Vermont | Singapore

CONTENTS

PART 2
Common Scenarios

PART 3
Key Names & Places

Introduction

Most people use fewer than 1,000 words of their first language every day. With just a vocabulary of a few hundred words, you'll be able to communicate a lot of ideas so as to socialize with the locals as well as to "survive" any situation you might find yourself in. ***Survival Arabic***'s approach is all about providing you with words, expressions and phrases commonly used in Arab socities, and supplying them both in helpful romanized transliteration and in Arabic characters. We hope this book helps you take the first step to communicating in Arabic with those who speak it.

How to Use This Book

There are at least ten different Arabic dialects used throughout the Arabic world, and although they belong to the same family, they can be as different as French, Italian, Spanish, and other Romance languages are from one another. These are bridged by Modern Standard Arabic (MSA), which all Arabs can use to communicate with each other, and it's what we've used in this book, with some colloquial phrases added in to help you along the way.

In addition to the Arabic characters, a transliteration using the familiar English alphabet is provided to help you pronounce the words, phrases, or sentences correctly. At the beginning of this book is an invaluable pronunciation guide, which explains how to pronounce the sounds—whereby you can use English as a guide to read out the Arabic letters—although nothing quite beats practicing with a native speaker to learn exactly how Arabic letters and sounds are pronounced.

Arabic Pronunciation

There are 28 letters in the Arabic alphabet, and their pronunciation is always the same, unlike the pronunciation of words like "car" and "cease."

THE ARABIC ALPHABET

All Arabic letters are consonants. Generally speaking the Arabic language does not have the same system as the English alphabet. Experts use the word "***abajad***" meaning that the writing system uses primarily consonants.

	Sounds like	Example
أ	'alif **a** as in "**a**rm"	أنا ***anaa*** "I"
ب	**b** as in "**b**at"	بلد ***balad*** "country"
ت	**t** as in "**t**o"	تدليك ***tadliik*** "massage"
ث	**th** as in "**th**ree"	ثلاثة ***thlaatha*** "three"
ج	**j** as in "**j**elly"	جميل ***jamiil*** "beautiful"
ح	**h** No English equivalent. An emphatic **h** sound, from the very back of the throat. Heavily aspirated.	حُب ***hob*** "love"
خ	**kh**, as in "**loch**"	خمسة ***khamsa*** "five"
د	**d** as in "**d**ebt"	دار ***daar*** "house"
ذ	**dh** as in "**th**ere"	ذَهَبَ ***dhahaba*** "to go"
ر	**r**, a rolled **r** sound	مرآة ***mir'aah*** "mirror"
ز	**z** as in "**z**oo"	زار ***zaara*** "visited"
س	**s** as in "**s**un"	ساعة ***saa'ah*** "hour"

ش	**sh** as in "**sh**ine"	شكرا ***shukran*** "thank you"
ص	**s** like **s**, but very heavily pronounced.	صديق ***sadiiq*** "friend"
ض	**d** like **d**, but very heavily pronounced.	ضابط ***daabit*** "officer"
ط	**t**, like **t**, very heavily pronounced. (similar to **T**okyo)	طفل ***tifl*** "child"
ظ	**z** Like **th or z** but very heavily (similar to "**th**ose")	ظهر ***zahr*** "back" pronounced
ع	' No English equivalent. Like **a** with a constriction of the throat.	عين ***'ayn*** "eye"
غ	**gh**, No English equivalent. An **r** in the back of the throat	غني ***ghaniy*** "rich"
ف	**f** as in "**f**ace"	فيل ***fiil*** "elephant"
ق	**q**, a **k** sound from deep in the back of the throat.	قُطن ***qutn*** "cotton"
ك	**k** as in "**k**ite"	كتاب ***kitaab*** "book"
ل	**l** as in "**l**ight"	ليمون ***laymoon*** "lemon"
م	**m** as in "**m**ango"	موز ***mawz*** "bananas"
ن	**n** as in "**n**uts"	نمل ***naml*** "ants"
ه	**h** as in "**h**ammer"	هلال ***hilaal*** "crescent moon"
و	**w** as in "**w**as"	وردة ***wardah*** "rose"
ي	**y** as in "**y**ellow"	يد ***yad*** "hand"

ARABIC VOWELS

In standard Arabic, there are three short vowels commonly called ***harakaat*** حركات and three long vowels called ***huruf al mad*** حروف المد.

Short vowels

These are indicated by adding small symbols, above or below the consonants they are to be pronounced to make the sounds "**a**," "**u**" or "**i**." However, such marks are usually only found in children's books or elementary level school books, and are omitted from modern adult texts, because educated Arabic speakers know the vowels from the context (so only the consonants are written out).

Sign	Sound in English	Example
َ (***fathah***) above the letter	**a** as in "**a**t"	***kataba*** كَتَبَ "to write"
ِ (***kasrah***) below the letter	**i** as in "**i**t"	***kitaab*** كِتاب "a book"
(***dammah***) ُ above the letter	**u** as in "p**u**t"	***kutub*** كُتُب "books"

In ***Survival Arabic***, short vowels and diacritics are written to prevent confusion, e.g., to differentiate "***Amman***" عَمان from عُمان "**Oman**" or to indicate the passive voice, e.g., the passive form of the word "to write" ***kataba*** كَتَبَ is written **kutiba** كُتِبَ.

Short vowels and diacritics are useful for learners, but once you know the language they are not needed. Apart from religious and poetry texts, Arabs rarely use short vowels (***h**arakaat*).

Long Vowels

The long vowels are written with normal letters from the Arabic alphabet and they are the same sounds as the short vowels, but twice as long. These three letters are called: ا ***alif*** الف, و ***waaw*** واو and ي ***yaa'*** ياء.

Sign	Sound in English	Example
ا	**aa** as in "f**a**r" but longer	أنا **anaa** "I"
ي	**ii** as in "s**ee**"	أمي **um-mii** "my mother"
و	**uu** as in "n**oo**n"	بيوت **boyoot** "houses"

SHADDA (DOUBLING OF CONSONANTS)

A double consonant is where the consonant is stressed, such as in "boo**kk**eeping or "u**nn**atural," e.g., مدرِّس **muda<u>rr</u>is** "teacher." In Arabic, this is denoted by a (ّ) شدّة ***sh**addah*.

MADDAH

A glottal stop, where the voice breaks like in "uh-oh" is denoted by a wavy line (~) ***maddah*** above the long vowel, e.g., (آ) **aa**, ***mir'aah*** مرآة "mirror" and ***qur'aan*** قرآن "Koran."

Introduction to the Arabic Script

Arabic is written and read from right to left in a cursive style. The letters must always attach to each other, otherwise they are considered to be meaningless. There are four different forms for the letters: the letter when written on its own, when appearing at the beginning, in the middle and at the end of a word. Only ا ***alif***, د ***daal***, ذ ***dhal***, ر ***raa'***, ز ***zay*** and و ***waaw***, connect from the right side and never with each other, e.g., ورود ***woroud*** "roses," دار ***daar*** "house," أراد ***arad*** "want," and زار ***zaara*** "visited."

There are two major script styles that are used in different Arab countries: Al-ruq'ah and Annaskh style (which is what this book uses). Al-ruq'ah الرقعة is a common handwriting style used mainly in the Eastern regions (Egypt, Lebanon, Jordan, Syria and the Gulf countries). People find it quicker and more convenient. Annaskh النسخ is typically used for printed books and newspapers, and is more popular in the North African regions, e.g., Algeria, Morocco and Tunisia.

A Brief Introduction to Arabic Grammar

PERSONAL PRONOUNS

I	***anna*** أنا
we	***nahnu*** نحن
you [fem.]	***anti*** أنتِ
you [masc.]	***anta*** أنتَ
you [pl., masc]	***antum*** أنتم
you [pl., fem]	***antun-na*** أنتن
you [dual*]	***antumaa*** أنتما

he	***huw a*** هو
she	***hiya*** هي
they [dual*]	***humaa*** هما
they [pl., masc.]	***hum*** هم
they [pl., fem.]	***hun-na*** هن

*Used when referring to two of anything.

POSSESSIVE PRONOUNS

A possessive adjective or pronoun agrees in gender and in number with the noun it refers to (the owner). The following table using the example كتاب ***kitaab*** (book) illustrates the way possessives are formed in Arabic:

my	***-i*** ـي	e.g., ***kitaabii*** كتابي "my book"
your [masc.]	***-ka*** ـكَ	e.g., ***kitaabuka*** كتابكَ "your book"
your [fem.]	***-ki*** ـكِ	e.g., ***kitaabuki*** كتابكِ "your book"
his	***-u*** ـه	e.g., ***kitaabuhu*** كتابه "his book"
her	***-haa*** ـها	e.g., ***kitaabuhaa*** كتابها "her book"
our [dual]	***-naa*** ـنا	e.g., ***kitaabunaa*** كتابنا "our book"
your [dual]	***-kumaa*** كما	e.g., ***kitaabukumaa*** كتابكما "your book"
their [dual]	***-humaa*** ـهما	e.g., ***kitaabuhuma*** كتابهما "their book"
your [masc.]	***-kum*** ـكم	e.g., ***kitaabukum*** كتابكم "your book"

your [fem.]	***-kunna*** ـكنّ	e.g., ***kitaabukun-na*** كتابكنّ "your book"
their [masc.]	***-hum*** ـهم	e.g., ***kitaabuhum*** كتابهم "their book"
their [fem.]	***-hunna*** ـهنّ	e.g., ***kitaabuhun-na*** كتابهنّ "their book"

GENDER IN NOUNS

In Arabic, nouns are either masculine or feminine. With most nouns, you can change the masculine form to the feminine form by adding the feminine marker suffix ***-ah***. For example:

English meaning	**Masculine**	**Feminine**
student	***ṯaalib*** طالب	***ṯaalibah*** طالبة
teacher	***mudarris*** مدرّس	***mudarrisah*** مدرّسة
principal/manager	***mudiir*** مدير	***mudiirah*** مديرة

Some nouns are inherently masculine or feminine and cannot be changed from one to the another. For example:

English meaning	**Masculine**	**Feminine**
boy	***walad*** ولد	
girl		***bint*** بنت
man	***rajul*** رجل	
woman		***imra'ah*** إمرأة

Note that even non-animated objects are assigned a gender as in the following examples. The main clue to gender is whether the noun has the ***-ah*** at the end or not.

house ***bayyt*** [masc.] بيت	city ***madiinah*** [fem.] مدينة
country ***balad*** [masc.] بلد	ruler ***masṯara*** [fem.] مسطرة
pen ***qalam*** [masc.] قلم	table ***ṯaawilah*** [fem.] طاولة

THE DEFINITE ARTICLE

The definite article "the" is marked by adding ***al-*** الـ before the noun as in the following examples:

walad	ولد	a boy	***al-walad***	الولد	the boy
bayt	بيت	a house	***al-bayt***	البيت	the house

DUAL AND PLURAL NOUNS

Arabic differentiates between dual and plural nouns although the dual form ان ***-aan*** is not frequently used. The dual and the regular plural ون -***uun*** can be derived from the singular form in the following manner:

	Singular	**Dual** ان ***-aan***	**Plural** ون ***-uun***
player	***laa`ib*** لاعِب	***laa`ibaan*** لاعبان	***laa'ibuun*** لاعبون
teacher	***mudarris*** مدرِّس	***mudarrisaan*** مدرّسان	***mudarrisuun*** مدرّسون
spectator	***mutafarrij*** متفرّج	***mutafarrijataan*** متفرِّجان	***mutafarrijuun*** متفرّجون

The above examples refer to the masculine gender only.

FEMININE DUAL AND PLURAL NOUNS

Replace the female marker ***-ah*** for the singular noun with the feminine dual تان ***-taan*** and the feminine plural feminine suffix ات ***-aat***. See the examples below:

	Singular	Dual تان *-taan*	Plural ات *-aat*
player	***laa`ibah***	***laa`ib-at-aan***	***laa'ibaat***
	لاعِبة	لاعبتان	لاعبات
teacher	***mudarrisah***	***mudarris-at-aan***	***mudarrisaat***
	مدرّسة	مدرّستان	مدرّسات
spectator	***mutafarrijah***	***mutafarrij-at-aan***	***mutafarrijaat***
	متفرّج	متفرّجان	متفرّجات

VERBS

There are two different types of verbs in Arabic depending on their tense: past (action complete) and present (action incomplete). Verbs are conjugated for person, number and gender.

PERSON

In Arabic the first, second and third persons verbs are conjugated as follows. Consider the following examples using the root verb دَرَسَ ***darasa***:

I study.	***anaa `adrusu***	أنا أدرس
You [sing., masc.] study.	***anta tadrusu***	أنتَ تدرس
You [sing., fem.] study.	***anti tadrusiin***	أنت تدرسين
He studies.	***huwa yadrusu***	هو يدرس
She studies.	***hiwa tadrusu***	هي تدرس

I studied.	***anaa darastu***	أنا درستُ
You [sing., masc.] studied.	***anta darasta***	أنتَ درستَ
you [sing., fem.] studied.	***anti darasti***	أنتِ درستِ
He studied.	***huwa darasa***	هو درس
She studied.	***hiwa darasat***	هي درسَتْ

GENDER IN VERBS

In both the past and present tenses, the verbs must differentiate between the masculine or feminine gender of the subject. The feminine gender verb ending is usually marked by a ***-t*** sound. The gender marking paradigm for past tense verbs is as follows:

The boy ate.	***al-waladu akala.***	الولد أكل
The girl ate.	***al-bintu akalat.***	البنت أكلت

Gender in present tense verbs is marked by adding prefixes ***ya*** and ***ta*** to signal male and female respectively:

The boy eats/is eating.	***al-waladu ya`kulu.***	الولد يأكل
The girl eats/is eating.	***al-bintu ta`kulu.***	البنت تأكل

In this book, [FEMALE] indicates that the phrase is spoken by a female speaker.

NEGATION

There are two ways to express negation in Arabic: one that follows nouns ***laysa*** ليس "not to be," and the other that precedes verbs ***laa*** لا "does not."

THE NEGATION WORDS *LASTU* AND *LAYSA* ليس "NOT (TO BE)"

This is always inserted after the noun, i.e., "She is not..." or "He is not... ." You can sometimes drop the pronoun, e.g., "I am not angry." ***Lastu ghaadiban.*** لستُ غاضباً. as the modified form of ***laysa***, ***lastu***, clearly indicates the subject "I." Here are the different forms of ***laysa*** with different pronouns:

I'm not	***anaa lastu***	أنا لستُ
we're not	***nahnu lasnaa***	نحن لسنا
you're [sing., masc.] not	***anta lasta***	أنتَ لستَ
you're [sing., fem.] not	***anti lasti***	أنتِ لستِ
you're not [dual] not	***antuma lastuma***	أنتمَا لستمَا
you're [pl., masc.] not	***antum lastum***	أنتم لستم
you're [pl., fem.] not	***antunna lastunna***	أنتنَّ لستنَّ
he's not	***huwa laysa***	هو ليس
she's not	***hiya laysat***	هي ليَسَتْ
they're [pl., masc.] not	***hum laysuu***	هم ليسوا
they're [pl., fem.] not	***hunna lasna***	هنّ لسن

VERBAL NEGATION WORDS

There are four words used to negate verbs in the present, past, the future and the continuing past tenses respectively. These are shown in the following examples:

Negation	Tense	Example	Meaning
laa لا	Present	***Laa ashrab.*** لا أشرب	I don't drink.
lan لن	Future	***Lan ashrab.*** لن أشرب	I won't drink.
lam لم	Past	***Lam ashrab.*** لم أشرب	I did not drink.
maa ما	Past/ Continuing	***Maa sharibtu.*** ماشربتُ	I haven't drunk.

Peace be upon you. As-salaamu `alaykum.
And upon you be peace. Wa `alayykumus salaam.
How are you? Kayfa haaluki?
I'm tired. Anaa ta`baanah.
I've been traveling. Kuntu musaafira(h).
How are you? Kayfa haaluki?
I'm well, thanks to God. Anaa bikhayr, Alhamdullah.

PART ONE
Everyday Phrases

Greeting Etiquette

As in most cultures, men shake hands. If two people keep holding each other's hands for a while after the initial handshake, it's a sign of friendship. Close friends, especially for women, may kiss on the cheeks (at least twice).

Conservative Muslims, especially in the Gulf countries, believe that unnecessary eye or physical contact (such as shaking hands) between unrelated men and women should be avoided. This should not be seen as disrespectful or unwelcoming; it's just that opposite sexes in these countries socialize differently from in the West, and physical contact with a female Muslim may be considered offensive. Also refrain from patting members of the opposite sex on their shoulders, arms or backs. In short, limit your physical contact with them until they indicate it's okay to do so.

Greetings

KEY WORDS AND EXPRESSIONS

hello	***ahlan***	أهلاً
good	***al khayr***	الخير
upon you	***`alaykum***	عليكم
peace	***as-salaam***	السلام
safety	***as-salamah***	السلامة
morning	***sabaah***	صباح
evening	***msaa'***	مساء
meeting	***liqa'***	لقاء
night	***layla***(h)	ليلة
day	***nahar***	نهار
welcome/Hi	***marhaba***	مرحبا
light	***an-nnour***	النور
(used when responding to a greeting)		
occasion	***fursa***	فرصة
happy [fem.]	***sa`iidah/masrurah***	سعيدة/ مسرورة
happy	***masrur/sa`iid***	مسرور/ سعيد
how	***kayfa***	كيف
thank you	***shukran***	شكراً
honored (pl.)	***tasharrafnaa***	تشرفنا
honored (sing.)	***tasharaftu***	تشرفت
too	***aydhan***	أيضاً

Peace be upon you.

The most common Arabic greeting is ***As-salaamu `alaykum*** السلام عليكم, an Islamic greeting that is used by Muslims and non-Muslims alike.

And upon you be peace. (Response to the previous greeting) ***Wa `alayykumus salaam.*** و عليكم السلام.

Hello. ***Marhaban.*** مرحباً.

Welcome. ***Ahlan wa sahlan.*** أهلاً وسهلاً.

Welcome to you. [TO A GROUP] ***Ahlan bikum.*** أهلاً بكم.
[MALE, SING.] ***Ahlan bika.*** أهلاً بكَ.
[FEMALE, SING.] ***Ahlan biki.*** أهلاً بكِ.

Good morning. ***Sabahul khayr.*** صباح الخير.
[RESPONSE] ***Sabahun nuur.*** صباح النور.

Good evening. ***Masaa'al khayr.*** مساء الخير.
[RESPONSE] ***Masaa`un nuur.*** مساء النور.

Not too bad. ***Laa ba`s.*** لا بأس.

It's been so long, hasn't it?
Laqad marra waqtun tawiil, alaysa kadhaalik?
لقد مر وقت طويل، أليس كذلك؟

I've been very busy.
[MALE] ***Kuntu mashghuulan jiddan.*** كنت مشغولاً جداً.
[FEMALE] ***Kuntu mashghula(h) jiddan.*** كنت مشغولة جداً.

I've been away. ***Kuntu musaafiran.*** كنت مسافراً.

I've been traveling. ***Kuntu musaafira(h).*** كنت مسافرة.

We've been traveling. *Kunna musaafiriin.* كنا مسافرين.

How are you? [MALE] *Kayfal haal?* كيف الحال؟
[MORE FORMAL] *Kayfa haaluka?* كيف حالكَ؟
[FEMALE] *Kayfa haaluki?* كيف حالكِ؟

I'm fine, thanks. *Anaa bikhayr, shukran.* أنا بخير، شكراً.

I'm well, Alhamdullah ("God be praised" or "thanks to God").
Anna bikhayr, alhamdullah. أنا بخير، الحمد لله.

I'm not very well. *Lastu `alaa maa yuraam.*
لست على ما يرام.

I'm tired. [MALE] *Anaa ta`baan.* أنا تعبان.
[FEMALE] *Anaa ta`baanah.* أنا تعبانة.

I'm angry. [FEMALE] *Anaa ghadbaanah.* أنا غضبانة.

I'm worried.
[MALE, COLLOQUIAL] *Anaa qaliq/qalaqaan.* أنا قلقان/قلق
[FEMALE, COLLOQUIAL] *Anaa qaliqah/qalaqaanah.*
أنا قلقانة /أنا قلقة

I'm happy. [MALE] *Anaa masrur/sa`iid.* أنا مسرور/سعيد.
[FEMALE] *Anaa masruurah/sa`iidah.* أنا مسرورة/سعيدة.

SOME REGIONAL COLLOQUIAL GREETINGS

* Certain colloquial expressions are specific to different parts of the Arabic-speaking world, and these are indicated in the text under the headings: Levant, Gulf and Egypt.

Levant:

How are you? [SING.] ***Kiif halalak?*** كيف حالك؟
[PL., SING.] ***kiifkom/Kiif ahwalkum?***
كيفكم/كيف أحوالكم؟

How are you? [MALE] ***Kiifak?*** كيفَك؟
[FEMALE] ***Kiifek?*** كيفِك؟

How's work? ***Kiifesh-shughl?*** كيف الشغل؟

How's everyone (in the family)**?** ***Kiifel-ahl?*** كيف الأهل؟

How's (your) **health?** ***Kiifes-sah-hah?*** كيف الصحة؟

How's everything? ***Kiifel-umuur?*** كيف الأمور؟

Everything is well, I hope (God willing)**?**
Umuurukum tayibah in-sha-Allah?
أموركم طيبة إن شاء الله؟

Gulf:

Welcome! (Very nice to see you) ***Halaa Wallah!***
هلا و الله!

I hope you're doing well (God willing)**!**
Tayibeen in-sha-Allah! طيبين إن شاء الله!

Egypt:

How're you? [SING.] ***Iz-zayyak?*** ازيك؟
[PL.] ***Izayukoom*** ازيكم؟

Good [MALE] ***Kwayyes*** كويس
[FEMALE] ***Kwayyesah*** كويسة

Pleased to meet you. ***Fursah sa'iidah.*** فرصة سعيدة.

Introductions

Arab people in the Gulf countries and the Levant (Eastern Mediterranean) region like to use titles when addressing people. In informal instances people address each other using "***abu***" or "***umu***" which means "father" or "mother (of)," paired with the first name of the person's eldest child, e.g., "father of Ahmed" ***abu Ahmed***. Also, Arabs from the same regions use titles such as ***Duktoor***, ***Ustadh*** or ***Bash mohandis*** to address people in highly respected professions.

KEY WORDS AND EXPRESSIONS

first name	***ism***	اسم
family name	***al-laqab/ al-ism al-`aa'ili***	اللقب/ الإسم العائلي
from	***min***	من
where	***ayna***	أين
city/town	***mediinah***	مدينة
country	***balad***	بلد
this	***hadha***	هذا
this [fem.]	***haadhihi***	هذه
friend	***sadiiq***	صديق
friend [fem.]	***sadiiqah***	صديقة
friends	***`asdiqaa`***	أصدقاء
colleague	***zamiil***	زميل
colleague [fem.]	***zamiilah***	زميلة
colleagues	***zumalaa`***	زملاء
Mister	***Say-yid***	سيّد
Sir	***Say-yidii***	سيّدي
Madam	***Say-yidah***	سيّدة
(my) lady	***say-yidatii***	سيّدتي
Miss	***Aanisah***	آنسة
professor	***ustadh***	أستاذ
professor [fem.]	***ustadhah***	أستاذة
president	***ra'iis***	رئيس
president [fem.]	***ra'iisah***	رئيسة
director/manager	***mudiir***	مدير
director/manager [fem.]	***mudiirah***	مُديرَة
doctor	***duktuur***	دكتور
doctor [fem.]	***duktuurah***	دكتورة

engineer	***muhandis***	مهندس
engineer [fem.]	***muhandisah***	مهندسة
mother	***um/waalidah***	أم/والدة
father	***ab/waalid***	أب/والد
son	***ibn***	ابن
daughter	***bint***	بنت
brother	***a<u>kh</u>***	أخ
sister	***u<u>kh</u>t***	أخت
husband	***zawj***	زوج
wife	***zawjah***	زوجة
student	***<u>t</u>aalib***	طالب
student [fem.]	***<u>t</u>aalibah***	طالبة
I.D. card	***bi<u>t</u>aaqah hawiyyah***	بطاقة هوية
	bi<u>t</u>aaqatut-tta`riif	بطاقة التعريف
student I.D.	***bi<u>t</u>aaqah <u>t</u>aalib***	بطاقة طالب

May I introduce myself?

Isma<u>h</u> lii `an `uqaddima nafsii lak?

اسمح لي أن أقدم نفسي لك؟

My name is ... *Ismii ...* ... اسمي

What's your name? [FORMAL, APPROXIMATE TRANSLATION]

[MALE] *Masmuk?* ما اسمكَ؟

[FEMALE] *Maasmuki* ما اسمكِ؟

Please introduce yourself to us.

[MALE] *Qaddim nafsaka lanaa law sama<u>h</u>t?*

قدم نفسك لنا لو سمحت؟

[FEMALE] *Qaddimii nafsaki lanaa law sama<u>h</u>tii?*

قدمي نفسك لنا لو سمحتِ؟

Nice to meet you. *Fur<u>s</u>ah sa`iidah.* فرصة سعيدة.

My pleasure. *'anaa 'as`ad.* أنا أسعد.

This is Mr ... *Haa<u>dh</u>a huwas-sayyid...* هذا هو السيد ...

This is Mrs ... *Haa<u>dh</u>ihis-sayyidah...* هذه السيدة ...

This is Miss. ... *Haa<u>dh</u>ihil-aanisah...* هذه الآنسة ...

I'm a student.

[MALE] *Anaa <u>t</u>aalib.* أنا طالب.
[FEMALE] *Anaa <u>t</u>aalibah.* أنا طالبة.

I am the English teacher.

[MALE] *Anaa ustaa<u>dh</u>/mudar-ris al-lu<u>gh</u>ah al-injli iziyah.* أنا أستاذ/مدرس اللغة الإنجليزية.
[FEMALE] *Anaa ustaa<u>dh</u>ah/mudar-risah al-lu<u>gh</u>ah al-injliiziyah.* أنا أستاذة/مدرسة اللغة الإنجليزية.

I am the new principal/manager.

[MALE] *Anaa al-mudiir al-jadiid.* أنا المدير الجديد.
[FEMALE] *Anaa al-mudiirah al-jadiidah.* أنا المديرة الجديدة.

I am your new colleague.

[MALE] *Anaa zamiiluka al-jadiidah.* أنا زميلك الجديد.
[FEMALE] *Anaa zamiilatuka al-jadiid.* أنا زميلتك الجديدة.

This is my father. *Haa<u>dh</u>aa 'abii.* هذا أبي.

Let me introduce my father (to you).
Ua`rifuka `ala abii. أعرفك على أبي.

This is my mother. *Ha<u>dh</u>ihi ummii.* هذه أمي.

This is my sister. *Ha<u>dh</u>ihi u<u>kh</u>tii.* هذه أختي.

This is my brother. *Haa<u>dh</u>aa a<u>kh</u>ii.* هذا أخي.

This is my son. *Haa<u>dh</u>aa ibnii.* هذا ابني.

This is my daughter. *Ha<u>dh</u>ihi ibnatii.* هذه ابنتي.

This is my husband. *Haa<u>dh</u>aa zawjii.* هذا زوجي.

This is my wife. *Ha<u>dh</u>ihi zawjatii.* هذه زوجتي.

This is my (school/university) classmate.
[MALE] *Haa<u>dh</u>aa zamilii (fi al-madrasah/al-kulliyah)*
هذا زميلي في المدرسة/هذا زميلي فى الكلية.
[FEMALE] *Ha<u>dh</u>ihi zamilatii (fi al-madrasah/al-kulliyah)*
هذه زميلتي في المدرسة/هذه زميلتي فى الكلية

This is my friend.
[MALE] *Haa<u>dh</u>aa sadiiqii.* هذا صديقي.
[FEMALE] *Ha<u>dh</u>ihi sadiiqatii.* هذه صديقتي.

Welcome. *Ahlan wa sahlan.* أهلاً و سهلاً.

Pleased/honored to meet you. *Ta<u>sh</u>arafnaa.* تشرفنا

Please come in. *Tafa<u>dd</u>al biddu<u>kh</u>uul.* تفضل بالدخول.

Please take a seat. *Tafa<u>dd</u>al bil-juluus.* تفضل بالجلوس.

Thanks a lot. *<u>Sh</u>ukran jaziilan.* شكراً جزيلاً.

Don't mention it/you're welcome.
Laa <u>sh</u>ukra `alla waajib. لا شكر على واجب.

Expressing Thank You

Thanks	*<u>Sh</u>ukran*	شكراً
Thank you	*<u>Sh</u>ukran lak*	شكراً لك
Thank you very much	*<u>Sh</u>ukran jaziilan*	شكراً جزيلاً

May Allah reward you (all the best).
Jazakum Allahu kul <u>kh</u>air. جزاكم الله كل خير.

Thank you for your hospitality.
<u>Sh</u>ukran `alaa<u>d</u>iyafatikum. شكراً على ضيافتكم.

Thank you for your generosity.
<u>Sh</u>ukran `alaa karamakum. شكراً على كرمكم.

SOME VERY COMMON COLLOQUIAL EXPRESSIONS:

May Allah reward you!
Yujziikum Allah! يجزيكم الله
Tikram! تِكرَم!

Thanks so much for the effort!

Ta`abnaakum ma`aanaa! تعبناكم معانا!

By Allah, you spared no effort!

Wallah maa qasrtum! و الله ما قصرتم!

May (Allah) reward you with good health!

Yatikum es-sahah! يعطيكم الصحة!

Thanks to you, I have had a wonderful evening.

Bifadlik kaana masaa'ii raa'i`an.
بفضلك كان مسائي رائعاً.

I appreciate your kindness.

`Uqadder lutfak. أُقَدِّر لُطفَك.

Thanks for the meal.

Shukran `alal-wajbah. شكراً على الوجبة.

Thanks for the drink.

Shukran `alal-mashruub. شكراً على المشروب.

Thanks, I've had enough.

Shukran laqad iktafayyt. شكراً لقد اكتفيت.

Thanks for your assistance.

Shukran `alal-musaa`adah. شكراً على المساعدة.

I'm very grateful. *Mamnuun lak.* ممنون لك.

Don't mention it, you're most welcome!

Laa shukr `alaa waajib! لا شكر على واجب!

Apologizing

KEY WORDS AND EXPRESSIONS

apologies	*al`afw*	العفو
excuse me	*al ma`dhirah*	المعذرة
Sorry!	*Aasif!*	آسف!

Sorry I made you wait.

Alma`dhirah yaa akhii, 'ana ta'akhartu `alaik.

المعذرة يا أخي، أنا تأخرت عليك.

I'm so sorry for being late.

Aasif jidan, 'anaa muta'akh-khir.

آسف جداً، أنا متأخر.

I am truly sorry for what has happened.

A`tadhiru kathiiran limaa hasal.

أعتذر كثيراً لما حصل.

I apologize on her behalf; she did not know.

Atlubu al`wafwa bismihaa fahiyya la takun ta`rif.

أطلب العفو باسمها فهي لم تكن تعرف.

Please forgive me but I will not be able to come today.

Saamihnii lan 'astatii` 'an aatiya al yawm.

سامحني لن أستطيع أن آتي اليوم.

Apologize for what you did!

I`tadhir limaa fa`altahu! أعتذر لما فعلته!

She does not want to accept my apologies.

In-nahaa laa turiidu 'an tataqabbala i`tidhaaraatii.
إنها لا تريد أن تتقبل اعتذاراتي.

I apologized as soon as I found out it was my mistake.

I`tadhartu aw-wal maa `araft 'annahu kana khtaun min-ni. اعتذرت أوّل ما عرفت أنه كان خطأ منّي.

I am sorry. [MALE] *'Anaa 'aasif.* أنا آسف.
[FEMALE] *'Anaa 'aasifah.* أنا آسفة.

I am terribly sorry.

'Anaa fii ghaayatil-'asaf. أنا في غاية الأسف.

Please forgive me.

[MALE] *'Arjuuka saamihnii.* أرجوكَ سامحني.
[FEMALE] *'Arjuuki saamihiinii.* أرجوك سامحيني.

I didn't mean it.

Lam a`nii dhalik./Lam aqsud dhalik.
لم أعن ذلك/لم أقصد ذلك.

I apologize. *'Anaa 'a`tadhir.* أنا أعتذر.

Please accept my apologies.

[MALE] *'Arjuu 'an taqbala i`tidhaarii.*
أرجو أن تقبل اعتذاري.

[FEMALE] ***'Arjuu 'an taqbalii i`tidhaarii.***
أرجو أن تقبلي أعتذري.

Saying Goodbye

Leaving

See you later. ***Ilal-liqaa'.*** إلى اللقاء.

Goodbye. ***Ma`as-salamah./Fi Amaanillah.***
مع السلامة/في أمان الله.

Have a good night. [MALE] ***Tusbih `alaa khayr.***
تصبح على خير.
[FEMALE] ***Tusbihiina `alaa khayr.*** تصبحين على خير.

Good night. ***Laylah sa`iidah.*** ليلة سعيدة.

See you tomorrow. [MALE] ***Araaka ghadan.*** أراكَ غداً.
[FEMALE] ***Araaki ghadan.*** أراكِ غداً.

See you later. [MALE] ***Araaka ba`da qalil.*** أراكَ بعد قليل.
[FEMALE] ***Araaki ba`da qalil.*** أراكِ بعد قليل.

Safe trip. ***Tareeq es-salaamah.*** طريق السّلامة.

See you next week.
[MALE] ***Araakal-`sbuu` al qaadim.*** أراكَ الأسبوع القادم.
[FEMALE] ***Araakil `usbuu` al qaadim.*** أراكِ الأسبوع القادم.

See you next year, God willing. Araaki es-sanah al muqbilah, Inshaa'Allah.
It's been a pleasure. Janet fursah sa'iida.
I hope we see you again. Ataman-naa an naraaki mar-ratan `ukhraa.
We'll meet again. God willing. Sanaltaqii marrah thaaniy-yah, Inshaa'Allah.
Goodbye! Ilaal-liqaa'.
Take care! Diiri baalik `alaa haalik.

Take care!

[MALE, COLLOQUIAL] ***Diir baalak `ala haalak!***
دير بالك على حالك!

[FEMALE, COLLQUIAL] ***Diirii balik `ala haalik!***
ديري بالِك على حالك!

I'm leaving tomorrow. I came to say goodbye.

[MALE SPEAKING TO A MALE] ***Anna dhaahib ghadan. Ji'tu lii'uwadi'uka.*** أنا ذاهب غداً. جئت لأودعك.

I'm leaving tomorrow. I came to say goodbye.

[FEMALE SPEAKING TO A FEMALE] ***Anna dhaahiba ghadan. Ji'tu lii'uwaddi'aki.*** أنا ذاهبة غداً. جئت لأودعك.

When are you traveling? We're really going to miss you!

Mataas-safar? Sanaftaqidukum kathiran!
متى السفر؟ سنفتقدكم كثيراً!

See you next year, God willing. [TO A MALE]

Araakaki [F] ***es-sanah al muqbilah, Inshaa'Allah.***
أراكَ السنة المقبلة، إن شاء الله.

See you next year, God willing. [TO A FEMALE]

Araaki es-sanah al muqbilah, inshaa'Allah.
أراكِ السّنة المقبلة، إن شاء لله.

See you tomorrow, God willing. [TO A GROUP]

Araakum ghadan, Inshaa'Allah.
أراكم غداً، إن شاء لله.

See you next week, God willing. [TO A FEMALE]
Araaki al'usbuu` al-qaadim inshaa'Allah.
أراكِ الأسبوع القادم، إن شاء لله.

It's been a pleasure. I hope we see you again. [TO A MALE]
Kaanat fursah sa`iidah. Ataman-naa an naraaka mar-ratan u`ukhra.
كانت فرصة سعيدة. أتمنى أن نراك مرة أخرى.

It's been a pleasure. I hope we see you again.
[TO A FEMALE] *Kaanat fursah sa`iidah. Ataman-naa an araaki mar-ratan'ukhraa.*
كانت فرصة سعيدة. أتمنى أن أراكِ مرة أخرى.

We'll meet again, God willing.
Sanaltaqii marrah thaaniy-yah, Inshaa'Allah.
سنلتقي مرة ثانية، إن شاء لله.

See you soon. *Araakum qariban.* [TO A GROUP]
أراكم قريباً.

Goodbye. *Wadaa`an.* وداعاً.

Take care. *Diir baalak `alaa haalak.*
دير بالك على حالك.

Look after yourself. *I`tani binafsik.* اعتنِ بنفسك.

See you. *`Ilal liqaa'.* إلى اللقاء.
Response to the above. *Ma`essalaamah.* مع السّلامة.

I don't like goodbyes. ***Laa `uhibbul-wadaa`.***
لا أحب الوداع.

"In Allah's protection"—an Islamic expression used to bid farewell to someone. ***Fii `amaanil-lah.*** في أمان لله.

Have a safe trip! ***Rafaqatkas -salaamah!*** رافقتك السّلامة!

Asking Questions

KEY WORDS AND EXPRESSIONS

is/have/has/ does/will etc.	***hal*** (for Yes/No questions)	هل؟
Who?	***Man?***	من؟
What?	***Maa?/ Maadha?***	ما/ ماذا؟
When?	***Mataa?***	متى؟
Where?	***Ayna?***	أين؟
How much/ How many?	***Kam?***	كم؟
How?	***Kayfa?***	كيف؟
Why?	***Limaa?/Limaadhaa?***	لما؟/لماذا؟
question	***su'aal***	سؤال
answer	***jawaab***	جواب
(to) whom?	***Liman?***	لمن؟
(with) whom?	***Ma`a man?***	مع من؟
Which?	***Ay-yu?***	أيّ؟
From where?	***Min ayna?***	من أين؟
Where ... to?	***Ilaa ayna?***	إلى أين؟
nationality	***jinsiyyah***	جنسيّة

Cheryl, where are you from? Cheryl, min 'ayna 'anti?
I am Australian. Anaa 'Ustraaliy-yah.
Where are we going? Ilaa 'ayna nahnu dhaahibuun?
Let's go to the market. Hayyaa nadhhab `ilas-suuq.
When does the market open? Mataa yaftahus-suuq?
It opens at 10am. As-saa`ah al 'aashira.
How can we get to the market? Kayfa nadhhabu `ilas-suuq?
Let's take a taxi. Bisiyaarat ujra/ bit-taaksii.
Okay. Tayib.

American	***Amiriikiyy*** [fem.]	أمريكيّ
	Amiriikiyya [fem.]	
Australian	***'Usturaaliyy***	أستراليّ
	'Ustraliiyya [fem.]	
British	***Briiṯaaniyy***	بريطانيّ
	Briiṯaniya [fem.]	
Canadian	***Kanadiyy***	كنديّ
	Kanadiyya [fem.]	
Chinese	***S̲iiniyy***	صينيّ
	S̲iiniiyyah [fem.]	
Dutch	***Hulandiyy***	هولنديّ
	hulandiiyya [fem.]	
French	***Faransiyy***	فرنسيّ
	Faransiyya [fem.]	
German	***Almaniyyah***	ألمانيّ
	Almaaniyya [fem.]	
country	***dawlah***	دولة
America	***Amriikaa***	أمريكا
Australia	***'Usturaalyaa***	أستراليا
Britain	***Briiṯaanyaa***	بريطانيا
Canada	***Kanadaa***	كندا
China	***As̲-S̲iin***	الصّين
France	***Faransaa***	فرنسا
Germany	***Almaanyaa***	ألمانيا
New Zealand	***Nyuuziilandah***	نيوزيلندا
Singapore	***Singhaafuurah***	سنغافورة
continent	***qaarrah***	قارّة
city	***madiinah***	مدينة
province	***muẖaafaz̲ah***	محافظة
state	***wilaayah***	ولاية

Regional Colloquial Expressions

Gulf:

How?	*Shlun?*	شلون؟
Why?	*Liish?*	ليش؟
From where?	*Min wiin?*	من وين؟

Levant:

How?	*Kiif?*	كيف؟
What?	*Shou?*	شو؟

Egypt:

How?	*Ez-zaay?*	إزاي؟
Why?	*Liih?*	ليه؟
Who?	*Miin?*	مين؟
Where?	*Fiin?*	فين؟

Are you Italian? *Hal anta `Iitaaliyy?* هل أنت إيطالي؟
[FEMALE] *Hal anti `Iitaaliyyah?* هل أنتِ إيطالية؟

No, I am Australian. *Laa, anaa 'usturaaliyy.*
لا ، أنا أسترالي.

Are you German? [FEMALE] *Hal anti Almaniy-yah?*
هل أنتِ ألمانية؟

Yes, I am. *Na`am, anaa Almaniyyah.*
نعم، أنا ألمانية.

Who are you? *Man anta?* من أنت؟

Who is that man? *Man dhaalikar-rajul?* من ذلك الرجل؟

Who speaks English here?
Man yatahaddathu al-Injliiziyyah hunaa?
من يتحدث الإنجليزية هنا؟

Whose car is this?
Sayyaaratu man haadhih? سيارة من هذه؟

Whose bags are those?
Haqaa`ibu man tilk? حقائب من تلك؟

Whom are you talking to?
Ma`a man tatakallam? مع من تتكلم؟

When does the market open?
Mataa yaftahus-suuq? متى يفتح السوق؟

When do you have to go?
Mataa yajibu an tadh-hab? متى يجب أن تذهب؟

Where is the restaurant? *'Aynal-mat`am?* أين المطعم؟

Where is the hotel? *'Aynal-funduq?* أين الفندق؟

Where are you from? *Min 'ayna 'anta?* من أين أنتَ؟
[FEMALE] *Min 'ayna 'anti?* من أين أنتِ؟

Where are we going? *'Ilaa 'ayna nahnu dhaahibuun?*
إلى أين نحن ذاهبون؟

Where do you want to go?
'Ilaa 'ayna turiidu an tadh-hab? إلى أين تريد أن تذهب؟

Where is the bus stop?
'Ayna mawqiful baas? أين موقف الباص؟

How much does this shirt cost?
Bi-kam haadhal-qamiis? بكم هذا القميص؟

How long will you stay here?
Kam satabqaa hunaa? كم ستبقى هنا؟

How long does the train trip to Cairo take?
Kam ta'khudhur rihlatu bilqitaar 'ilal-qaahirah?
كم تأخذ الرحلة بالقطار إلى القاهرة؟

How are you? *Kayfa haaluk?* كيف حالك؟

How can I get to the market?
Kayfa yumkin an adh-haba 'ilas-suuq?
كيف يمكن أن أذهب إلى السوق؟

Counting and Numbers

THE CARDINAL NUMBERS

0	*sifr*	٠
1	*waahid*	١
2	*ithnaan*	٢

3	*thalaathah*	٣
4	*arba`ah*	٤
5	*khamsah*	٥
6	*sittah*	٦
7	*sab`ah*	٧
8	*thamaaniyah*	٨
9	*tis`ah*	٩
10	*`asharah*	١٠
11	*a-hada `ashar*	١١
12	*ithnaa `ashar*	١٢
13	*thalaathata `ashar*	١٣
14	*'arba`ata `ashar*	١٤
15	*khamsata `ashar*	١٥
16	*sittata `ashar*	١٦
17	*sab`ata `ashar*	١٧
18	*thamaaniyata `ashar*	١٨
19	*tis`ata `ashar*	١٩
20	*`ishruun*	٢٠
21	*waahid wa `ishruun*	٢١
22	*ithnaan wa `ishruun*	٢٢
24	*'arba`ah wa `ishruun*	٢٤
26	*sittah wa `ishruun*	٢٦
28	*thamaaniyah wa `ishruun*	٢٨
30	*thalaathuun*	٣٠
40	*'arba`uun*	٤٠
50	*khamsuun*	٥٠
60	*sittuun*	٦٠
70	*sab`uun*	٧٠
80	*thamaanuun*	٨٠
90	*tis`uun*	٩٠
100	*mi'ah*	١٠٠

101	*mi'ah wa waahid*	١٠١
103	*mi'ah wa thalaathah*	١٠٣
105	*mi'ah wa khamsah*	١٠٥
107	*mi'ah wa sab`ah*	١٠٧
108	*mi'ah wa thamaaniyah*	١٠٨
109	*mi'ah wa tis`ah*	١٠٩
110	*mi'ah wa `asharah*	١١٠
120	*mi'ah wa `ishruun*	١٢٠
130	*mi'ah wa thalaathuun*	١٣٠
140	*mi'ah wa 'arba`uun*	١٤٠
150	*mi'ah wa khamsuun*	١٥٠
160	*mi'ah wa sittuun*	١٦٠
170	*mi'ah wa sab`uun*	١٧٠
180	*mi'ah wa thamaanuun*	١٨٠
190	*mi'ah wa tis`uun*	١٩٠
200	*mi'ataan*	٢٠٠
201	*mi'ataan wa waahid*	٢٠١
300	*thalaathu mi'ah*	٣٠٠
400	*'arba`u mi'ah*	٤٠٠
500	*khamsu mi'ah*	٥٠٠
600	*sittu mi'ah*	٦٠٠
700	*sab`u mi'ah*	٧٠٠
800	*thamaanu mi'ah*	٨٠٠
900	*tis`u mi'ah*	٩٠٠
1,000	*'alf*	١٠٠٠
1,500	*alf wa khamsu mi'ah*	١٥٠٠
2,000	*alfaan*	٢٠٠٠
3,000	*thalaathat 'aalaaf*	٣٠٠٠
4,000	*arba`at 'aalaaf*	٤٠٠٠
5,000	*khamsat 'aalaaf*	٥٠٠٠

6,000	***sittat 'aalaaf***	٦٠٠٠
7,000	***sab`at 'aalaaf***	٧٠٠٠
8,000	***thamaaniyat 'aalaaf***	٨٠٠٠
9,000	***tis`at 'aalaaf***	٩٠٠٠
10,000	***`ashrat 'aalaaf***	١٠٠٠٠
11,000	***a-hada `ashara 'alf***	١١٠٠٠
12,000	***'ithnaa `ashara 'alf***	١٢٠٠٠
17,000	***sab`ata `ashara 'alf***	١٧٠٠٠
100,000	***mi'at 'alf***	١٠٠٠٠٠
250,000	***rub`u milyuun***	٢٥٠٠٠٠
500,000	***nisf milyuun***	٥٠٠٠٠٠
1,000,000	***milyuun***	١٠٠٠٠٠٠

number	***raqam***	رقم
numbers	***arqaam***	أرقام
how many/much	***kam***	كم
account	***hisaab***	حساب
accounts	***hisaabaat***	حسابات
percentage	***mi'awiya***	مئوية
count	***`ad***	عد
division	***qismah***	قسمة
multiplication	***darb***	ضرب
big/large (number)	***kabiir***	كبير
small (number)	***saghiir***	صغير

THE ORDINAL NUMBERS

first	***'awwal***	أول
second	***thaanii***	ثاني
third	***thaalith***	ثالث
fourth	***raabi`***	رابع

fifth	***kh*aamis**	خامس
sixth	***saadis***	سادس
seventh	***saabi`***	سابع
eighth	***th*aamin**	ثامن
ninth	***taasi`***	تاسع
tenth	***`ashir***	عاشر
eleventh	***haadii `ashar***	حادي عشر
twelfth	***thanii `ashar***	ثاني عشر
thirteenth	***thaalith `ashar***	ثالث عشر
fourteenth	***raabi` `ashar***	رابع عشر
fifteenth	***khaamis `ashar***	خامس عشر

NOTE A number used as a modifier needs to agree with the noun in gender and number (feminine, masculine, singular and plural).

Who is first?

[GROUP, MALE] ***Man huwaal-awwal?***
من هو الأول؟
[GROUP, FEMALE] ***Man hiwa al 'uulaa?***
من هي الأولى؟

Which one is first?

Maa huwa ash-shay' al-awwal? ما هو الشيء الأول؟

Who is last?

[MALE] ***Man huwa al-akhiir?*** من هو الأخير؟
[FEMALE] ***Man hiya al-akhirah?*** من هي الأخيرة؟

Which is last? ***Maa huwa al-akhiir?*** ما هو الأخير؟

Counting Things

Feminine and masculine forms of numbers

Numbers 1 and 2 come *after* the nouns they modify and *need to agree* with the noun in gender.

1 [masc.]	***waahid***	واحد
1 [fem.]	***waahidah***	واحدة
2 [masc.]	***ithnaan***	اثنان
2 [fem.]	***ithnataan***	اثنتان

I have one brother and two sisters.
`indii 'akhun waahid wa 'ukhtaan ithnataan.
عندي أخ واحد و أختان اثنتان.

The numbers from 3–10 ***precede*** the noun they describe and ***disagree*** with it in gender, that is, if the noun they modify is masculine, the numbers are feminine.

3 [masc.]	***thalaath***	ثلاث
3 [fem.]	***thalaathah***	ثلاثة
4 [masc.]	***'arba`***	أربع
4 [fem.]	***'arba`ah***	أربعة
5 [masc.]	***khams***	خمس
5 [fem.]	***khamsah***	خمسة
6 [masc.]	***sitt***	ست
6 [fem.]	***sittah***	ستة
7 [masc.]	***sab`***	سبع
7 [fem.]	***sab`ah***	سبعة
8 [masc.]	***thamaan***	ثمان
8 [fem.]	***thmaaniyah***	ثمانية
9 [masc.]	***tis`***	تسع

Ahmed, how many siblings do you have? Ahemd kam ikhwa `indek?
I have three sisters and five brothers. `Indii thalaathu 'akhawaat wa arba`atu `ikhwah.
How about you? Wa anta?
I have one brother and two sisters. `Indii 'akh waahid wa 'ukhtaan ithnataan.
Do you have any children? Hal `indak awalaad?
Yes, I have three daughters. N`am, `indii thalaath banaat.
How old are they? Kam a`maruhum?
They are eight, seven and five years old. Thamaaniyah wa sab`a wa khamsa.

9 [fem.]	*tis`ah*	تسعة
10 [masc.]	*`ashr*	عشر
10 [fem.]	*`ashrah*	عشرة

I have three daughters.
`Indii thalaathu banaat. عندي ثلاث بنات.

I invited four of my (male) friends for dinner.
Da`awtu 'arba`atan min asdiqaa'ii `alal `ashaa'.
دعوت أربعة من أصدقائي على العشاء.

I have three sisters and five (male) brothers.
`Indii thalaathu 'akhawaat wa arba`atu `ikhwah.
عندي ثلاث أخوات و أربعة إخوة.

I have one car.
'Indii siy-yarah waahidah. عندي سيارة واحدة.

She has two books. *`Indahaa kitabayn.* عندها كتابين.

I have four rooms (in my house).
Fii baytii arb`u ghuraf. في بيتي أربع غرف.

I have visited five cities so far.
Zurtu khamsa mudun lihad-di al-aan.
زرت خمس مدن لحد الآن.

There are six men in this café.
Yuujad sittatu rijaal fii hadhaa al-maqhaa.
يوجد ستة رجال في هذا المقهى.

I work with seven women.

A`malu ma` sab`i nisaa'. أعمل مع سبع نساء.

There are eight students in the classroom.

Yuujaduu thmaaniyatu tullab fii ghufatis-saf.

يوجد ثمانية طلاب في غرفة الصف.

Eight candidates are competing for the first position.

Tis`atu murash-shahiin yatanafasuuna `alal-mansibil-awwal. تسعة مرشحين يتنافسون على المنصب الأول.

The drink is for ten Dinars.

Si`ru al-mashroub `asharata danaaniir.

سعر المشروب عشرة دنانير.

Expressing Time

KEY WORDS AND EXPRESSIONS

time	*al waqt*	الوقت
hour	*saa`ah*	ساعة
hours	*saa`aat*	ساعات
minute	*daqiiqah*	دقيقة
minutes	*daqaai'q*	دقائق
second	*thaanyah*	ثانية
seconds	*thwaanii*	ثواني
midnight	*muntasaf al-layl*	منتصف الليل
a.m.	*sabaahan*	صباحاً
p.m.	*masaa'an*	مساءً
early	*mubakkiran*	مبكراً
late	*muta'akh-khir*	متأخر

appointment	*maw`id*	موعد
before	*qabla*	قبل
after	*ba`da*	بعد
during	*'athnaa'*	أثناء
noon	*zuhr*	ظهر
afternoon	*ba`da az-zuhr*	بعد الظهر
the hour	*as-saa`ah*	الساعة
watch/clock	*saa`a*	ساعة
quarter	*rub`*	ربع
half	*nisf*	نصف
from ... to	*min... 'ilaa*	من... إلى
past	*wa*	و
to	*il-laa*	إلا

What time is it?	*Kam as-saa`ah?*	كم الساعة؟
It is 1 o'clock now.	*As-saa`atu. al'aan alwaahidah.*	الساعة الآن الواحدة.
2 o'clock	*ath-thaaniyah*	الثانية
3 o'clock	*ath-thaalithah*	الثالثة
4 o'clock	*ar-raabi`ah*	الرابعة
5 o'clock	*al-khaamisah*	الخامسة
6 o'clock	*as-saadisah*	السادسة
7 o'clock	*as-saabi`ah*	السابعة
8 o'clock	*ath-thaaminah*	الثامنة
9 o'clock	*at-taasi`ah*	التاسعة
10 o'clock	*al-`aashirah*	العاشرة
11 o'clock	*al-haadiyata `ashrata*	الحادية عشرة
12 o'clock	*ath-thaaniyata `ashrata*	الثانية عشرة

five past one	*alwaahidah wa khams daqaa'iq*	الواحدةو خمس دقائق
ten past two	*ath-thaaniyah wa `ashr daqaa'iq*	الثانية و عشر دقائق
quarter past five	*al-khaamisah war-rub`*	الخامسة و الربع
twenty past two	*ath-thaaniyah wath-thuluth*	الثانية و الثلث
half past seven	*as-saabi`ah wan-nisf*	السابعة و النصف
quarter to nine	*at-taasi`ah 'illa rub`*	التاسعة إلا ربع
twenty to ten	*al-`aashirah 'illa thuluth*	العاشرة إلا ثلث
ten to eleven	*al-haadiyata `asharata 'illaa `ashara daqaa'iq*	الحادية عشرة إلا عشر دقائق
1 minute	*daqiiqah*	دقيقة
2 minutes	*daqiiqataan*	دقيقتان
3 minutes	*thalaath daqaa'iq*	ثلاث دقائق
4 minutes	*arba` daqaa'iq*	أربع دقائق
5 minutes	*khams daqaa'iq*	خمس دقائق
6 minutes	*sitt daqaa'iq*	ست دقائق
7 minutes	*sab` daqaa'iq*	سبع دقائق
8 minutes	*thamaan daqaa'iq*	ثمان دقائق
9 minutes	*tis` daqaa'iq*	تسع دقائق
10 minutes	*`ashr daqaa'iq*	عشر دقائق
quarter of an hour	*rub` saa`ah*	ربع ساعة
half an hour	*nisf saa`ah*	نصف ساعة
hour and a half	*saa`ah wa nisf*	ساعة و نصف
2 hours	*saa`ataan*	ساعتان

3 hours	*thalaath saa`aat*	ثلاث ساعات
4 hours	*arba` saa`aat*	أربع ساعات
5 hours	*khams saa`aat*	خمس ساعات
6 hours	*sitt saa`aat*	ست ساعات
7 hours	*sab` saa`aat*	سبع ساعات
8 hours	*thamaanii saa`aat*	ثماني ساعات
9 hours	*tis` saa`aat*	تسع ساعات
10 hours	*`ashr saa`aat*	عشر ساعات
24 hours	*'arba` wa `ishruun saa`ah*	أربع و عشرون ساعة
36 hours	*sittah wa thalaathuun saa`ah*	ستة و ثلاثون ساعة
72 hours	*ithnaan wa sab`uun saa`ah*	اثنان و سبعون ساعة

What time is it now? *Kamis-saa`tul-aan?* كم الساعة الآن؟

What time are we leaving?
Mataa sanughaadir? متى سنغادر؟

What time does the bus leave?
Mataa yughaadirul baas? متى يغادر الباص؟

What time is breakfast? *Matal-'iftaar?* متى الإفطار؟

What time is lunch? *Matal-ghadaa'?* متى الغداء؟

What time is dinner? *Matal-`ashaa'?* متى العشاء؟

One moment, please! *Lahzah min fadlik!* لحظة من فضلك!

What time does the museum open?

Mataa yaftahul muthaf? متى يفتح المتحف؟

What time does the movie start?

Mataa yabda'ul-film? متى يبدأ الفيلم؟

Are you busy after 7:00 p.m.?

Hal 'anta mashghuul ba`das-saabi`ah?

هل أنت مشغول بعد السابعة؟

Yes, I am. *Na`am 'anaa mashghuul.* نعم، أنا مشغول.

What time is the departure?

Matal-mughadarah? متى المغادرة؟

It is at 5:30 a.m. *Fil-khaamisati wannisf sabaahan.*

في الخامسة و النصف صباحاً.

What time is your appointment?

Mataa maw`iduk? متى موعدك؟

Will this take long?

Hal saya'khudhu dhaalika waqtan tawiilan?

هل سيأخذ ذلك وقتاً طويلاً؟

I think it will take about half an hour.

'Azunnu 'annahu saya'khudh nisf saa`ah taqriiban.

أظن أنه سيأخذ نصف ساعة تقريباً.

I will be back shortly. *Sa'a`uudu qariiban.* سأعود قريباً.

I will be back in 10 minutes.

Sa'a`uudu ba`da `ashari daqaa'iq.

سأعود بعد عشر دقائق.

I will try to finish it in an hour.

Sa'uhaawilu an antahiya minhu fii saa`ah.

سأحاول أن أنتهي منه في ساعة.

If I have time, I would like to go to Dubai.

'Arghabu fidh-dhahaabi `ilaa dubay `idhaa kaana `indii waqt. أرغب في الذهاب إلى دبي إذا كان عندي وقت.

It's late, isn't it?

Alwaqtu muta'akh-khir, 'alayysa kadhaalik?

الوقت متأخر، أليس كذلك؟

It is still early. *Alwaqtu laa yazaalu mubakkiran.*

الوقت لا يزال مبكراً.

Sorry, I am late.

'Aasif, anaa muta'akh-khir. آسف، أنا متأخر.

Times of the Day

KEY WORDS AND EXPRESSIONS

dawn	*fajr*	فجر
morning	*sabaah*	صباح
daytime	*nahaar*	نهار
afternoon	*`asr*	عصر
dusk	*maghrib*	مغرب

evening	*masaa'*	مساء
night	*layl*	ليل
midnight	*muntasafil-layl*	منتصف الليلْ
today	*al-yawm*	اليوم
tomorrow	*ghadan*	غداً
yesterday	*'ams*	أمس
day after tomorrow	*ba`da ghad*	بعد غد
day before yesterday	*maa qablal-'ams*	ما قبل الأمس
every day	*kulla yawm*	كلّ يوم
day after day	*yawm ba`da yawm*	يوم بعد يوم
in the morning	*fis-sabaah*	في الصباح
in the afternoon	*fiz-zuhr*	في الظهر
this evening	*haadhal massaa'*	هذا المساء
tonight	*al-laylah*	الليلة
tomorrow morning	*ghadan sabaahan*	غداً صباحاً
every morning	*kulla sabbah*	كلّ صباح
every day	*kulla yawm*	كلّ يوم
every night	*kulla layylah*	كلّ ليلة
from now on	*minal 'aan*	من الآن
	fasaa`idan	فصاعداً
now	*al 'aan*	الآن
immediately	*fawran/*	فوراً/
	`alaa al-fawr	على الفور
later	*fiimaa ba'd*	فيما بعد
eve	*fii `ashiyati*	في عشية
lately	*muakh-kharan*	مؤخراً
formerly/previously	*saabiqan*	سابقاً
sometime	*fii waqtin maa*	في وقت ما
shortly	*ba`da qaliil*	بعد قليل
in a day/a day later	*ba`da yawm*	بعد يوم

in two days/ two days later	*ba`da yawmayn*	بعد يومين
not yet	*laysa ba`d*	ليس بعد
(it) is still	*maa zaala*	مازال
forever	*ilaa al-abad*	إلى الأبد
never	*abadan*	أبدًا
always	*daa'iman*	دائمًا
continuously	*bistimraar*	باستمرار
one moment	*lahdhah*	لحظة
one minute	*daqiiqah*	دقيقة
an hour later/ after an hour	*Ba`d saa`ah*	بعد ساعة

From now on, I will wake up early.

Sa-as-hu baakiran minal yawmi fasaa`idan.

سأصحو باكراً من اليوم فصاعداً.

Every morning I walk for half an hour.

Kul sabaah amshii limuddat nisf saa`ah.

كل صباح أمشي لمدة نصف ساعة.

I will drink the coffee later.

Sa-ashrab al qahwah fiimaa b`ad.

سأشرب القهوة فيما بعد.

I like to watch the sun set every evening.

Uhibbu mushaahadah ghuruub ash-shams kul masaa'.

أحب مشاهدة غروب الشمس كل مساء.

I work every morning and every afternoon.

A`malu sabaaha wa `ashiyata kul yaum.

أعمل صباح و عشية كل يوم.

The weather is always beautiful here.

At-taqsu jamiil daa'iman hunaa. الطقس جميل دائماً.

We hear the train every night.

Nasma`u al qitaar kul laylah. نسمع القطار كل ليلة.

I ride the bus to work every day.

Arkabu al haafilah 'ilaa ash-shughl kul yawm.

أركب الحافلة إلى الشغل كل يوم.

She will leave the office shortly.

Satughaadiru al maktab b`da qaliil.

ستغادر المكتب بعد قليل.

I drink water constantly because it is very hot.

Ashrabul-maa' bistimraar li'anna al jaw haarr jidan. أشرب الماء باستمرار لأن الجو حار جدا.

The trip will be for tomorrow morning.

Assafar sayakuun ghadan sabaahan.

السفر سيكون غداً صباحاً.

The new director/manager will come next week.

Saya'tii al mudiir al jadiid al usbuu` al qaadim.

سيأتي المدير الجديد الأسبوع القادم.

The report was ready since yesterday.
At-taqriir jaahiz mun<u>dh</u>u yawm al ams.
التقرير جاهز منذ يوم الأمس.

Wait a minute please, I'm talking on the phone.
La<u>hz</u>a min fa<u>d</u>lik anaa ata<u>h</u>ad-da<u>th</u>u `alaa al haatif.
لحظة من فضلك، أنا أتحدث على الهاتف.

The line is still busy.
Al <u>kh</u>a<u>t</u> maa zaala ma<u>shgh</u>ulan. الخط ماز ال مشغولاً.

The price has changed lately.
Ta<u>gh</u>ay-yar as-si`r mu'a<u>kh</u>aran. تغيّر السّعر مؤخراً.

Days and Weeks

KEY WORDS AND EXPRESSIONS

day	*yawm*	يوم
days	*ay-yaam*	أيام
week	*usbuu`*	أسبوع
weeks	*asaabii`*	أسابيع
days of the week	*ay-yaam al usbuu`*	أيام الأسبوع
the next day	*al-yaum at-taalii*	اليوم التالي
the day before	*al-yaum as-saabiq*	اليوم السابق
in a few days	*fii bi<u>d</u>` ati ay-yaam*	في بضعة أيام
during two days	*<u>kh</u>ilaal yawmain*	خلال يومين

NOTE When we indicate the day we precede it by the word *yaum*. e.g., **Monday** *yaumul-i<u>th</u>nain*.

Saturday	*Assabt*	السّبت
Sunday	*Al-ahad*	الأحد
Monday	*Al-ithnayn*	الاثنين
Tuesday	*Ath-thulaathaa'*	الثّلاثاء
Wednesday	*Al-'arbi`aa'*	الأربعاء
Thursday	*Al-khamiis*	الخميس
Friday	*Al-jum`ah*	الجمعة
from Saturday	*min Assabt*	من السبت
until Monday	*ilaal-ithnayyn*	إلى الاثنين

What day of the week is today?
Ayyu yawmin minal-usbou`i alyawm?
أي يوم من الأسبوع اليوم؟

Today is Monday. *Alyawm huwal ithnayn.* اليوم هو الاثنين.

I am going to Cairo on Wednesday.
Sa'adh-habu 'ilal-qahirah yawmal arba`aa'.
سأذهب إلى القاهرة يوم الأربعاء.

I will return to Dubai on Friday afternoon.
Sa'a`uudu 'ilaa dubay ba`da zuhri yawmil jum`a.
سأعود إلى دبي بعد ظهر يوم الجمعة.

I have a meeting on Thursday.
`Indii ijtimaa` yawmal-khamiis.
عندي اجتماع يوم الخميس.

See you next Thursday.
'Araakal-khamiis alqaadim. أراك الخميس القادم.

I am going to see the pyramids this Sunday.
Sa'ushahidul-'ahramaat yawmal 'ahad.
سأشاهد الأهرامات يوم الأحد.

Counting Days

KEY WORDS AND EXPRESSIONS

one day	*yawm waahid*	يوم واحد
two days	*yawmaan*	يومان
three days	*thalaathata 'ayyaam*	ثلاثة أيام
four days	*arba`ata 'ayyaam*	أربعة أيام
five days	*khamsata 'ayyaam*	خمسة أيام
six days	*sittatata 'ayyaam*	ستة أيام
seven days	*sab`ata 'ayyaam*	سبعة أيام
eight days	*thamaaniyata 'ayyaam*	ثمانية أيام
nine days	*tis`ata 'ayyaam*	تسعة أيام
ten days	*`ashrata 'ayyaam*	عشرة أيام
eleven days	*'ahada `ashara yawman*	أحد عشر يوماً
fourteen days	*arba`ata `ashara yawman*	أربعة عشر يوماً
twenty days	*`ishruun yawman*	عشرون يوماً
thirty days	*thalaathuun yawman*	ثلاثون يوماً
forty days	*'arba`uun yawman*	أربعون يوماً
several days	*`iddata 'ayyaam*	عدة أيام
a few days	*'ayyaam qaliilah*	أيام قليلة
the first day	*al-yawm al-awwal*	اليوم الأول
the second day	*al-yawm ath-thanii*	اليوم الثاني
the third day	*al-yawm ath-thaalith*	اليوم الثالث

the fourth day	*al-yawm ar-rabi`*	اليوم الرابع
the fifth day	*al-yawm al-khaamis*	اليوم الخامس
the sixth day	*al-yawm as-saadis*	اليوم السادس
the seventh day	*al-yawm as-saabi`*	اليوم السابع
the eighth day	*al-yawm ath-thaamin*	اليوم الثامن
the ninth day	*al-yawm at-taasi`*	اليوم التاسع
the tenth day	*al-yawm al-`aashir*	اليوم العاشر
the eleventh day	*alyawm al-haadi `ashar*	اليوم الحادي عشر
the twelth day	*al-yawm ath-thaani `ashar*	اليوم الثاني عشر
the thirteenth day	*al-yawm ath-thaalith `ashar*	اليوم الثالث عشر
the fourteenth day	*al-yawm ar-raabi` `ashar*	اليوم الرابع عشر
the fifteenth day	*al-waym al-khaamis `ashar*	اليوم الخامس عشر
the twentieth day	*al yawm al `ishruun*	اليوم العشرون
the thirtieth day	*al-yawm ath-thalaathun*	اليوم الثلاثون
the fortieth day	*al-yawm al-arba`uun*	اليوم الأربعون
the fiftieth day	*al-yawm al-khamsuun*	اليوم الخمسون
the sixtieth day	*al-yawm as-situun*	اليوم الستون
the seventieth day	*al-yawm as-sab`uun*	اليوم السبعون
the eightieth day	*al-yawm ath-thamaanuun*	اليوم الثمانون
the ninetieth day	*al-yawm at-tis`uun*	اليوم التسعون

How many days are we going to stay in Casablanca?
Kam yawm sanabqaa fid-daaril-baydaa'?
We are going to stay there for five days.
Sanabaqaa hunaaka khamsat ay-yaam.
I will take a few days off (work).
Sa`aakhudh `utlaa minal`amal libid`ati ayyam.
When are you going to Abu Dhabi?
Mataa satadhhabiin 'laa 'abuu zabii?
I will go in two weeks.
Sa'adhhab b`adaa asbu`ayan.
How many days will you spend there?
Kam yawm satumdiin hunaak?
I will spend four days (there).
Sa`umdii 'arba`ata 'ayyaam hunaak.

the hundredth day *al-yawm al-mi'ah* اليوم المئة

How many days are we going to stay in Casablanca?
Kam yawman sanabqaa fid-daaril-baydaa'?
كم يوماً سنبقى في الدار البيضاء؟

I am going to stay there for ten days.
Sa'abqaa hunaak li`ashrati ayyaam.
سأبقى هناك لعشرة أيام.

I will take a few days off.
Sa'u`attil ayyaam qaliilah. سأعطّل أياماً قليلة.

How many days will you spend there?
Kam yawman satumdii hunaak? كم يوماً ستمضي هناك؟

I will spend four days.
Sa'umdii 'arba`ata 'ayyaam. سأمضي أربعة أيام.

How many days till the end of the year?
Kam yawman baqiya linihayat es-sanah?
كم يوماً بقى لنهاية السنة؟

I have a few days left to graduate!
Baqiyat ayaam qaliilah qablat-takharruj!
بقيت أيام قليلة قبل التخرج!

It's just five days till New Year Eve.
Baquiyat khamsatu ay-yaamin `alaa ra'si es-sanah.
بقيت خمسة أيام على رأس السنة.

Just a few days to (our) summer vacation!

Baqiyat ay-yaam qaliila `alaa `utlatis-sayf!

بقيت أيام قليلة على عطلة الصيف!

It will take many more days to reach (our destination).

Baqiyat `iddatu ay-yaam `alaa wusuulina.

بقيت عدة أيام على وصولنا.

We will come back in a few days.

Sanarji` ba`da bid`ati ay-yaamin.

سنرجع بعد بضعة أيام.

I will stay a few days.

Sa'abqaa bida`ta ay-yaamin. سأبقى بضعة أيام.

How many days are left till your birthday?

[MALE] *Kam yawman baqiya `ala `eid milaadika?*

كم يوماً بقي على عيد ميلادكَ؟

[FEMALE] *Kam yawman baqiya `ala `eid milaadiki?*

كم يوماً بقي على عيد ميلادكِ؟

How many days do you fast in Ramadaan?

Kam yawman tasuumu fii ramadaan?

كم يوماً تصوم في رمضان؟

Weeks and Weekends

It varies, but many Arab countries consider the weekend to be on Fridays and Saturdays, e.g., UAE, Egypt and Iraq. Other countries like Iraq may have just one weekend day—Friday.

KEY WORDS AND EXPRESSIONS

week	*usbuu`*	أسبوع
weeks	*'asaabii`*	أسابيع
two weeks	*usbuu`ayn*	أسبوعين
weekly	*usbuu`iyan*	أسبوعياً
weekly [adj., fem.]	*usbuu`iy-yah*	أسبوعية
every week	*kulla usbuu`in*	كل أسبوع
bi-weekly	*kulla usbuu`ayn*	كل أسبوعين
during the week	*khilaala al-usbuu`*	خلال الأسبوع
within the week	*fii bahri usbuu`in*	في بحر أسبوع
this week	*haadhaa al-usbuu`*	هذا الأسبوع
next week	*al-usbuu` al-qaadim*	الأسبوع القادم
last week	*al-usbuu` al-madii*	الأسبوع الماضي
at the end of the week	*`inda nihayatil-usbuu`*	عند نهاية الأسبوع
weekend	*`utlat nihaayat al-'usbuu`*	عطلة نهاية الأسبوع
from next week	*minal-usbou`il-qaadim*	من الأسبوع القادم
until next week	*hattal-usbou`il-qaadim*	حتى الأسبوع القادم

I am going to Amman this week.

Anaa dhaahibun 'ilaa `ammaan haadhal-'usbuu`.

أنا ذاهب إلى عمان هذا الأسبوع.

I need these documents next week.

'Ahtaaju haadhihil-wathaa'iq al'usbuu`al-qaadim.

أحتاج هذه الوثائق الأسبوع القادم.

You need to write a weekly report.

[MALE] ***Ta<u>h</u>taju an taktuba taqriiran kulla usbuu`.***
تحتاج أن تكتب تقريراً كل أسبوع.

[FEMALE] ***Tahtajiin an taktubii taqriiran kulla usbuu`.***
(أنتِ) تحتاجين أن تكتبي تقريراً كل أسبوع.

I have to write the weekly report.

`Alay-ya an aktuba at-taqriir al-usbuu`iy.
عليّ أن أكتب التقرير الأسبوعي.

This is a weekly magazine.

Haa<u>dh</u>ihii majal-lah usbuu`iy-yah.
هذه مجلة أسبوعية.

From next week on we will start working on a new project. ***Minal-usbuu` al-qaadim fa<u>s</u>aa`idan sanabda'ul-`amala `alaa ma<u>sh</u>ruu`in jadiidin.***
من الأسبوع القادم فصاعداً سنبدأ العمل على مشروع جديد.

I'll see you on the weekend.

[MALE] ***Sa'araaka fii `utlat nihayatil-usbuu`.***
سأراكِ في عطلة نهاية الأسبوع.

[FEMALE] ***Sa'araaki fii `utlat nihayatil-usbuu`.***
سأراكَ في عطلة نهاية الأسبوع.

We will meet again in two weeks.

Sanataqaabal mar-ratan <u>th</u>aaniya/u<u>kh</u>raa ba`da usbuua`ayn. سنتقابل مرة ثانية/أخرى بعد أسبوعين.

I arrived a week ago. ***Wasaltu min usbuu`in waahid.***
وصلت من أسبوع (واحد).

The accident happened last week.
Hadath al-haadith khilaal al-usbuu` al-maadii.
حدث الحادث خلال الأسبوع الماضي.

The delegation will arrive by the end of the week.
Saya'tii al-wafd `inda nihaayati al-usbuu`.
سيأتي الوفد عند نهاية الأسبوع.

The contract will end in these coming weeks.
Sayanatahii al-`aqd khilaal/fii al-asaabii` al-qaadimah.
سينتهي العقد خلال/في الأسابيع القادمة.

Counting Weeks

KEY WORDS AND EXPRESSIONS

one week	***'usbuu` waahid***	أسبوع واحد
two weeks	***'usbuu`ayn***	أسبوعين
three weeks	***thalaathat 'asaabii`***	ثلاثة أسابيع
four weeks	***'arba`at 'asaabii`***	أربعة أسابيع
five weeks	***khamsat 'asaabii`***	خمسة أسابيع
six weeks	***sittat 'asaabii`***	ستة أسابيع
seven weeks	***sab`atu 'asaabii`***	سبعة أسابيع
eight weeks	***thamaaniyat 'asaabii`***	ثمانية أسابيع
nine weeks	***tis`at 'asaabii`***	تسعة اسابيع
ten weeks	***`ashrat 'asaabii`***	عشرة أسابيع
twenty weeks	***`ishruuna 'usbuu`***	عشرون أسبوع

fifty-two weeks	*ithnaan wa khamsuun 'usbuu`*	اثنان و خمسون أسبوع
two weeks ago	*qabla 'usbuu`ayn*	قبل أسبوعين
three weeks later	*ba`da thalaathat 'asaabii`*	بعد ثلاثة أسابيع
a few weeks later	*ba`da 'asaabii` qaliilah*	بعد أسابيع قليلة

I arrived in Dubai two weeks ago.

Wasaltu 'ilaa Dubayy qabla 'usbuu`ayn.

وصلت إلى دبي قبل أسبوعين.

I will stay in Tunisia for three more weeks.

Sa'abqaa fii Tuunis lithalaathati 'asaabii` 'ukhraa.

سأبقى في تونس لثلاثة أسابيع أخرى.

I am going back in three weeks' time.

Sa'a`uudu khilaala sittati 'asaabii`.

سأعود خلال ستة أسابيع.

I would like to extend my reservation for one more week.

Awaddu an 'umaddida hajzii 'usbuu`an.

أود أن أمدّد حجزي أسبوعاً.

The prescription is for eight weeks.

Al-wasfah li-thamaaniyati asaabii`.

الوصفة لثمانية أسابيع.

The work will take more than...weeks.

Al-`amal sa-yastaghriq akthar min...asaabii`.

العمل سيستغرق أكثر من...أسابيع.

My mission will be completed in a few weeks.

Muhimmatii satantahii ba`da asaabii` qaliilah.

مهمّتي ستنتهي بعد أسابيع قليلة.

The new year will start in two weeks.

Satabda'u as-sanah al-jadiidah ba`da usbuu'ayn.

ستبدأ السنة الجديدة بعد أسبوعين.

Call me back in three weeks.

It-tasil bii thaaniyatan ba`da araba`ati asaabii`.

اتصل بي ثانية بعد أربعة أسابيع.

He took leave for ten weeks.

Akhadha `utlat `amal limud-dat `ashrati asaabii`.

أخذ عطلة عمل لمدة عشرة أسابيع.

The project will take many weeks.

Al-mashruu` saya'khudh `iddat 'asaabii`.

المشروع سيأخذ عدة أسابيع.

It will take many more weeks to finish the project.

Saya'khudh 'asaabii` `adiidah ukhraa li-injaaz al-mashruu`. سيأخذ أسابيع عديدة أخرى لإنجاز المشروع.

The patient will leave the hospital in a week.

Al-mariid sayughaadir al-mustashfaa khilaal usbuu` waahid. المريض سيغادر المستشفى خلال أسبوع واحد.

The Months of the Year

KEY WORDS AND EXPRESSIONS

month	*shahr*	شهر
months	*shuhuur/ash-hur*	شهور/أشهر
next month	*ash-shahr al-qaadim*	الشهر القادم
this month	*haadhaa ash-shar*	هذا الشهر
last month	*ash-shahr al-madii*	الشهر الماضي
every month	*kull shahr*	كل شهر
monthly	*shahriyan*	شهرياً

CALENDARS IN THE ARAB WORLD

Generally, two different calendars are used—the Islamic lunar calendar and the Western solar calendar. Some Arab or Islamic countries use the Hijrii (Islamic lunar) calendar in remembrance of Prophet Muhammad's migration from Mecca to Medina. The first day in this calendar was in the lunar month of Muharram, which corresponded with July 16, 622 CE. This date represents a turning point in the history of Islam's birth and rise and so marks the beginning of the Muslim era or calendar. The months according to the *Hijrii calendar are listed on page 70.

Notes:

*The Hijrii calendar is an Islamic lunar calendar—there are 354 or 355 days in a year in this lunar calendar, with an average of 29 or 30 days per month. There is a difference of 10 days from the Western (Gregorian) calendar, meaning that the annual holidays (e.g. Eid al Fitr) occurs earlier each year. Muslims use the Hijrii calendar to determine the dates for important events (e.g. Ramadaan, pilgrimages, etc.).

THE MONTHS OF THE HIJRII CALENDAR

1. ***Mu<u>h</u>arram***	محرمُ
2. ***<u>S</u>afar***	صفر
3. ***Rabii` al-aw-wal***	ربيع الأول
4. ***Rabii` a<u>th</u>-<u>th</u>aanii***	ربيع الثاني
5. ***Jamaadi al-aw-wal***	جمادى الأول
6. ***Jamaada a<u>th</u>-<u>th</u>aanii***	جمادى الثاني
7. ***Rajab***	رجب
8. ***<u>Sh</u>a`baan***	شعبان
9. ***Rama<u>d</u>aan***	رمضان
10. ***<u>Sh</u>awwaal***	شوّال
11. ***<u>Dh</u>uu al-qa`dah***	ذو القعدة
12. ***<u>Dh</u>uu al-<u>h</u>ijjah***	ذو الحجّة

THE MONTH OF *Rama<u>d</u>aan*

Muslims believe that during the month of ***Rama<u>d</u>aan***, Allah revealed the first verses of the Quran, the holy book of Islam to the prophet Mu<u>h</u>ammad, around 610 CE. Muslims practice ***<u>s</u>awm*** صوم, or fasting, for the entire month of ***Rama<u>d</u>aan***. This means that they abstain from eating, drinking, sexual intercourse and generally any sinful behavior from sunrise till sunset. During ***Rama<u>d</u>aan*** and in most Muslim countries most restaurants are closed during the day. Families get up early for ***su<u>h</u>uur*** سحور, a meal eaten before dawn. After sunset, the fast is broken with a meal known as ***iftaar*** إفطار.

THE MONTH OF *Shawwaal*

Ramaḏaan ends with a three-day festival of `*Iid al-fiṭr* عيد الفطر (or more commonly Eid al-Fitr) beginning on the first day of *Shawwaal*. At `*Iid al-fiṭr* people pray *ṣalatu al 'iid/ Eid* ('iid/Eid Prayer), dress in their best clothes, adorn their homes with lights and decorations, give treats to children, and exchange visits with friends and family.

THE PILGRIMAGE MONTH

In the twelfth month of the Islamic calendar, *Dhul-ḥijjah* ذو الحجة, Muslims perform the *Hajj* الحج, the pilgrimage to Mecca in Saudi Arabia. The *Hajj* is considered one of the five pillars of Islam, and every able-bodied Muslim should endeavor to make the journey at least once in their lifetime—although you may be exempted on grounds of hardship or ill health. Its annual observance corresponds with the major holy day `*Iid al'aḏ-ḥaa* عيد الأضحى, the second Islamic festival that may extend from one to four days in commemoration of Abraham's readiness to sacrifice his son, Ismaa`el, following divine orders. The *Hajj* is a series of extensively detailed rituals that include wearing a special garment that symbolizes unity and modesty.

THE WESTERN CALENDAR

This calendar is based on the Gregorian calendar and is called *attaqwiim almiilaadiy* التقويم الميلادي in reference to the birth of Christ. The abbreviation '*m*' م is used to denote it in written schedules, etc.

Today is Monday, 13 Rabi ath-thaani, 1439 (1st of January 2018 AD.)

Alyawm huwa alithnayn ath-thaalith `ashar rabi`uth-thaanii sanata 'alfin wa 'arbau mi'ah wa tis`u wa thlaathuun hijrii, al-khaamis min yanaayir sanata 'alfayn wa thamaaniyata `ashar.

اليوم هو الإثنين ١٣ ربيع الثاني ١٤٣٩ ه ، ١ يناير ٢٠١٨ م.

THE MONTHS OF THE WESTERN CALENDAR

The names of the months of the Western calendar vary within Arab countries. In the eastern areas of the region, the names of the indigenous Babylonian-Semitic months are still in use, whereas in Egypt and North African countries, the Gregorian names of the months along with the Babylonian are used.

January	*Yanaayir*	يناير
February	*Fibraayir*	فبراير
March	*Maars*	مارس
April	*Abriil*	أبريل
May	*Maayu*	مايو
June	*Yuunyu*	يونيو
July	*Yuulyu*	يوليو
August	*Ughustus*	أغسطس
September	*Sibtimbar*	سبتمبر
October	*'Uktuubar*	أكتوبر
November	*Nufambar*	نوفمبر
December	*Diisimbar*	ديسمبر

The Babylonian-Semitic months are:

January	***Kanuun ath-thaani***	كانون الثّاني
February	***Shubaat***	شباط
March	***Aadhaar***	آذار
April	***Niisaan***	نيسان
May	***Ayyaar***	أيار
June	***Huzayyraan***	حزيران
July	***Tamuuz***	تموز
August	***Aab***	أب
September	***Ayluul***	أيلول
October	***Tishriin al-awwal***	تشرين الأوّل
November	***Nufambar***	تشرين الثّاني
December	***Kanuun al-awwal***	كانون الأوّل

My birthday is next month.
`Iid miilaadii ash-shahral-qaadim.
عيد ميلادي الشهر القادم.

Are you going to be in Beirut in January?
Hal satakuunu fii Bayruut fii Yanaayer?
هل ستكون في بيروت في يناير؟

Counting Months

KEY WORDS AND EXPRESSIONS

Which day?	***Ay-yu yawam fii ash-shahr?***	أي يوم في الشهر؟
Which month?	***Ay-uu shahr?***	أي شهر؟
In what month?	***Fii ay-yii shahr?***	في أي شهر؟
How many months?	***Kam shahr?***	كم شهر؟

one month	*shahr waahid*	شهر واحد
two months	*shahrayyn*	شهرين
three months	*thalaathat shuhuur*	ثلاثة شهور
four months	*'arba`at shuhuur*	أربعة شهور
five months	*khamsat shuhuur*	خمسة شهور
six months	*sittat shuhuur*	ستة شهور
seven months	*sab`at shuhuur*	سبعة شهور
eight months	*thamaaniyat shuhuur*	ثمانية شهور
nine months	*tis`at shuhuur*	تسعة شهور
ten months	*`ashrat shuhuur*	عشرة شهور
twelve months	*ithnaa `ashara shahran*	اثنا عشر شهراً
a few months	*'ash-hur qaliilah*	أشهر قليلة
several months	*`iddat shuhuur*	عدة شهور

DAY

1st	*al'awwal*	الأول
2nd	*ath-thaanii*	الثاني
3rd	*ath-thaalith*	الثالث
4th	*ar-raabi`*	الرابع
5th	*al-khaamis*	الخامس
6th	*as-saadis*	السادس
7th	*as-saabi`*	السابع
8th	*ath-thaamin*	الثامن
9th	*at-taasi`*	التاسع
10th	*al`aashir*	العاشر
11th	*al-haadii `ashar*	الحادي عشر
12th	*ath-thaani `ashar*	الثاني عشر
13th	*ath-thaalith `ashar*	الثالث عشر
14th	*ar-raabi` `ashar*	الرابع عشر

15th	*al-khaamis `ashar*	الخامس عشر
16th	*as-saadis `ashar*	السادس عشر
17th	*as-saabi` `ashar*	السابع عشر
18th	*ath-thaamin `ashar*	الثامن عشر
19th	*at-taasi` `ashar*	التاسع عشر
20th	*al`ishruun*	العشرون
21st	*al-haadii wal`ishruun*	الحادي و العشرون
22nd	*ath-thaanii wal`ishruun*	الثاني و العشرون
23rd	*ath-thaalith wal`ishruun*	الثالث و العشرون
24th	*ar-raabi` wal`ishruun*	الرابع و العشرون
25th	*al-khaamis wal`ishrun*	الخامس و العشرون
26th	*as-saadis wal`ishruun*	السادس و العشرون
27th	*as-saabi` wal`ishruun*	السابع و العشرون
28th	*ath-thaamin wal`ishruun*	الثامن و العشرون
29th	*at-taasi` wal`ishruun*	التاسع و العشرون
30th	*ath-thalaathuun*	الثلاثون
31st	*al-haadii wath-thalaathuun*	الحادي و الثلاثون

How many months are you going to be here?
Kam shahran satabqaa hunaa? كم شهراً ستبقى هنا؟

I will be in Lebanon for two months.
Sa'abqaa fii Lubnaan li-shahrayyn.
سأبقى في لبنان لشهرين.

The project will take several months to finish.
Sayastaghriqul mashruu` `iddata ash-hur.
سيستغرق المشروع عدة أشهر.

What day is it today?
Maa taarikhul-yawm? ما تاريخ اليوم؟

It's the 5th. *Al-khaamis.* الخامس.

Tomorrow will be the 6th.
Ghadan sayakuunus-saadis. غداً سيكون السادس.

I was born on July 27th.
Wulidtu fis saabi` wal `ishriin min yuulyu.
ولدت في السابع و العشرين من يوليو.

Tomorrow will be the 20th of June.
Ghadan sayakuunul `ishriin min yuunyu.
غداً سيكون العشرين من يونيو.

I am leaving on the 14th of May.
Sa'ughaadiru fir-raabi` `ashar min maayu.
سأغادر في الرابع عشر من مايو.

I want these documents by the 20th of August.
'Uriidu haadhihil wathaa'iq qablal-`ishriin min 'ughustus. أريد هذه الوثائق قبل العشرين من أغسطس.

The Years

KEY WORDS AND EXPRESSIONS

year	*sanah/`aam*	سنة/عام
this year	*haadhihis-sanah*	هذه السنة
last year	*as-sanah al-maadiyah*	السنة الماضية
next year	*as-sanah al-qaadimah*	السنة القادمة

every year	*kul sanah*	كل سنة
new year	*sanah jadiidah*	سنة جديدة
for one year	*Waahid*	لعام واحد
year and a half	*`aam wa nisf*	عام و نصف
for three years	*li-thalaathati a`waam*	لثلاثة أعوام
Happy New Year	*`Aam sa`iid*	عام سعيد
New Year's Eve	*Laylat ra's as-sanah*	ليلة رأس السنة
years	*sanawaat/a`waam*	سنوات/أعوام
for a number of years	*li-sanawaat `adiidah*	لسنوات عديدة
for many years	*li-snawaat tawiilah*	لسنوات طويلة
Which year?	*Ayyi sana*	أيّ سنة؟
how many years?	*kam sanah*	كم سنة؟
from this year on	*min hadhihis-sanah/ min haadhal-`aam fasaa`idan*	من هذه السنة/ من هذا العام فصاعداً
yearly	*sanayy/sanawiyyah*	سنويّ/سنويّة
every year	*kol sanah/'aam*	كل أخرى/من عام إلى آخر
year to year	*min samah 'ilaa ukhraa/min 'aamin ilaa aakhar*	من سنة إلى أخرى/ من عام إلى آخر

I have studied Arabic for two years.
Darastu al`arabiyyah li`aamayn.
درست العربية لعامين.

I came to Syria this year. *Ji'tu 'ilaa suuryaa haadhal-`aam.*
جئت إلى سوريا هذا العام.

I was there last year. ***Kuntu hunaak al`aam al-maadii.***
كنت هناك العام الماضي.

Happy anniversary! ***Kul `aam wa anta bi-khayr!***
كل عام و أنت بخير!

This building is ancient; it was built many years ago.
Haadha al-mabnaa qadiim; buniya min sanawaatin `adiidah. هذا المبنى قديم، بني من سنوات عديدة.

2000	***'alfaan***	ألفان
2010	***'alfaan wa `asharah***	ألفان و عشرة
2011	***'alfaan/alfiin wa 'a-hada `ashar***	ألفان/ألفين و أحد عشرة
2015	***'alfaan/alfiin wa khamsata `ashar***	ألفان/ألفين وخمسة عشر
2016	***'alfaan/alfiin wa sittata `ashar***	ألفان/ألفين وستة عشر`
2017	***'alfaan/alfiin wa sab`ata `ashar***	ألفان/ألفين و سبعة عشر
2018	***'alfaan/alfiin wa thamaaniyat `ashar***	ألفان/ألفين و ثمانية عشر
2019	***'alfaan/alfiin wa tis`ata `ashar***	ألفان/ألفين و تسعة عشر
2020	***'alfaan wa `ishruun/`ishriin***	ألفين وعشرون عشرين

I was born in 1974.
Wulidtu `aam alf wa tis`umi'ah wa arba`ah wa sab`iin. ولدت عام ألف و تسعمئة و أربعة و سبعين.

I have been working for this company since August 2004.
A`malu fii haadhihish-sharikah mundhu ughustus `aam alfayyn wa arba`ah.
أعمل في هذه الشركة منذ أغسطس عام ألفين و أربعة.

Age

KEY WORDS AND EXPRESSIONS

age	*`umr/sin*	عمر/سن
child	*tifl*	طفل
adult	*baaligh*	بالغ
elderly person	*`ajuuz*	عجوز
young	*saghiir**	صغير
young [fem.]	*saghiirah*	صغيرة
old	*kabiir**	كبير
old [fem.]	*kabiirah*	كبيرة
young man	*shaab*	شاب
young woman	*shaabbah*	شابة
old woman	*`ajuuzah*	عجوز
old man	*shaikh*	شيخ

* In Arabic, ***saghiir*** is the word for young and small. Similarly, ***kabiir*** is the word for old (people) and big. (Old for non-human entities is ***qadiim***.)

How old are you?
Kam `umruk/ma sinnuk? كم عمرك؟/ما سنك؟

I am 31 years old. *`Umrii waahid wa thalaathuun sanah.*
عمري واحد و ثلاثون سنة.

My daughter is four years old.
`Umr ibnatii arba` sanawaat. عمر ابنتي أربع سنوات.

The new manager is very young.
Al muudir al jadiid saghiir as-sin.
المدير الجديد صغير السن.

The fortress is very old. *Al qal`ah qadiimah jidan.*
القلعة قديمة جداً.

The babysitter is too young.
Al haadinah saghirah jiddan fiis-sinni.
الحاضنة صغيرة جداً في السن.

The secretary is really young.
Mudiiratul-maktab jidu saghirah.
مديرة المكتب جد صغيرة.

My children are still young.
Awlaadii kulluhum sighaarus-sin.
أولادي كلهم صغار السن.

We have to take care of the elderly.
Yajibu 'an nahtam bikibaaris-sin.
يجب أن نهتم بكبار السن.

Age doesn't matter. *As-sin laa yahum-mu abadan.*
السن لا يهمّ أبداً.

There is is no age limit for this position.

Laa yujadu h̲ad lis-sin lihaad̲h̲aa al-mans̲ib.

لا يوجد حد للسن لهذا المنصب.

There is an age limit for the position.

Yuujad h̲ad lis-sin lihaad̲h̲aa al mans̲ib.

يوجد حد للسن لهذا المنصب.

He finished school at a very early age.

Intahaa minad-diraasah fi `umr mubakkir.

انتهى من الدراسة في عمر مبكر.

Seasons of the Year

KEY WORDS AND EXPRESSIONS

season/seasons	*fas̲l/fus̲uul*	فصل\فصول
seasons of the year	*fus̲uul as-sanah*	فصول السنة
four seasons	*al fus̲uul al-arba`aa*	الفصول الأربعة
winter	*(fas̲l) as̲h̲-s̲h̲itaa'*	(فصل) الشتاء
spring	*(fas̲l) ar-rabii`*	(فصل) الربيع
summer	*(fas̲l) as̲-s̲ayf*	(فصل) الصيف
autumn	*(fas̲l) al-k̲h̲ariif*	(فصل) الخريف

There are four seasons in the year.

Yuujad arba`tu fus̲uul fis-sanah.

يوجد أربعة فصول في السنة.

What is your favorite season?

[MALE] *Maa huwa al fas̲lu al mufad̲-d̲al `indaka?*

ما هو الفصل المفضل عندكَ؟

[MALE] ***Maa huwa fas̲luka al mufad̲-d̲al?***
ما هو فصلكَ المفضل؟
[FEMALE] ***Maa huwa al fas̲lu al mufad̲-d̲al `indaki?***
ما هو الفصل المفضل عندكِ؟
[FEMALE] ***Maa huwa fas̲luki al mufad̲-d̲al?***
ما هو فصلكِ المفضل؟

What are your favorite seasons?
Maa hiya al fus̲uul al mufad̲-d̲alah `indaka/`indaki?
ما هي الفصول المفضلة عندكَ/عندكِ؟
Maa hiya fus̲uluka/fus̲uluki al mufad̲-d̲alah?
ما هي فصولكَ/فصولكِ المفضلة؟

What is the best season in…?
Maa huwa afd̲alu fas̲l fii…? ما هو أفضل فصل في...؟

When does summer begin?
Mataa yabda'us sayf? متى يبدأ الصيف؟

Is it very cold during winter?
Halit̲-t̲aqsu baaridun jiddan at̲h̲naa'as̲h̲-s̲h̲itaa'?
هل الطقس بارد جداً أثناء الشتاء؟

What is the highest temperature in Riyadh?
Maa hiya darajatul-h̲araarah alqus̲waa fii Ar-riyaad̲?
ما هي درجة الحرارة القصوى في الرياض؟

What is the lowest temperature in the winter?
Maa hiya aqall/adnaa darajat h̲araarah fiis̲h̲-s̲h̲itaa'?
ما هي أقل/أدنى درجة حرارة في الشتاء؟

Does it rain in the winter?

Hal tasqutu al amtaar fii fasl ash-shitaa'?

هل تسقط الأمطار في فصل الشتاء؟

Does it snow in the winter?

Hal yasqut ath-thalj fii fasl ash-shitaa'?

هل يسقط الثلج في فصل الشتاء؟

Does it rain in the spring? *Hal tasqutu al amtaar fir-rabii`?*

هل تسقط الأمطار في الربيع؟

Is it windy during the fall season?

Hal yujadu riy-yaah khilala fasl al-khariif?

هل يوجد رياح خلال فصل الخريف؟

Are there any storms in…? *Hal tahduth 'awasif fii …?*

هل تحدث عواصف في …؟

What is the highest temperature in the summer?

Maa hiwa a`laa/aqsaa darajatu haraarah fis-sayf?

ما هي أعلى/أقصى درجة حرارة في الصيف؟

Talking about the Weather

KEY WORDS AND EXPRESSIONS

the weather	*al jaw/at-taqs*	الجو/الطقس
temperature	*darajat al-haraarah*	درجة الحرارة
weather forecast	*annashrah al-jawwiyyah*	النشرة الجوية
sun	*shams*	شمس

What is the weather like today? Kayfa huwaṯ-ṯaqsul yawm?
It is cold. 'Innahu baarid.
Do we need umbrellas? Hal sanaḫtaaj 'ilaa mizallaat?
Yes, it's raining outside. N`am, 'innahaa tumṯiru fil khaarij.
We'd better bring a jacket too. Wa Aydan, minal-afdal 'an na'khudh m`anaa al m`aaṯif.

sunny	*mushmis*	مشمس
cold	*barad/baarid*	برد/بارد
hot	*haarr*	حار
moderate	*mu`tadil*	معتدل
changing (adj.)	*mutaqallib*	متقلب
humid	*ratib*	رطب
dry	*jaaff*	جاف
wind/winds	*riih/riyaah*	ريح/رياح
storm	*`aasifah*	عاصفة
cloud	*ghaim/ghuyuum*	غيم/غيوم
cloudy	*ghaa'im*	غائم
fog	*dabaab*	ضباب
foggy	*dabaabiy*	ضبابي
rain	*matar*	مطر
rainy	*maatir/mumtir*	ماطر/ممطر
snow	*thalj*	ثلج
ice	*jaliid*	جليد
icy	*jaliidiy*	جليدي
frosting	*saqii`*	صقيع
hail	*barad*	برد
freezing (adj.)	*mutajammid*	متجمد
jacket/coat	*mi`taf*	معطف
gloves	*quf-fazaat*	قفازات
umbrella	*mizallah shamsiy-yah*	مظلة
sunglasses	*naz-zaara*	نظارة شمسية
hat	*qub-ba`ah*	قبعة

What is the weather like today?

Kayfa hwat-taqsul-yawm? كيف هو الطقس اليوم؟

It is hot. *'Innahu haarr.* إنه حار.

It is cold. *'Innahu baarid.* إنه بارد.

Where can I buy a raincoat?
Ayna yumkinunii 'an 'ashtarii mi`taf matar?
أين يمكنني أن أشتري معطف مطر؟

I don't like humid weather.
Laa 'uhibbul-jawwar-ratib. لا أحب الجوّ الرّطب.

Will it rain tonight?
Hal satumtirul-laylah? هل ستمطر الليلة؟

It's raining outside.
'Innahaa tumtiru fil-khaarij. إنها تمطر في الخارج.

It's raining heavily.
'Innahaa tumtiru bi ghazaarah. إنها تمطر بغزارة.

Do I need an umbrella? *Hal sa'ahtaaju 'ilaa mizallah?*
هل سأحتاج إلى مظلة؟

It's sunny today.
Aljaw mushmis al-yawm. الجوّ مشمس اليوم.

It is cloudy and cold.
Al-yawm ghaa'im wa baarid. اليوم غائم و بارد.

Does it snow in the south?

Hal yasqutu ath-thalj fil junuub?

هل يسقط الثلج في الجنوب؟

It does not rain much in this area.

Laa tumtir kathiiran fii haadhihi al-mintaqah.

لا تمطر كثيراً في هذه المنطقة.

This is hail, not snow.

Haadhaa barad wa laysa thalj. هذا برد و ليس ثلج.

A currency exchange counter at an airport.

PART TWO
Common Scenarios

Money

KEY WORDS AND EXPRESSIONS

money	*daraahim/fuluus/ amwaal*	دراهم/فلوس/ أموال
currency	*`umlah*	عملة
Australian dollar	*dulaar 'Usturaaliyy*	دولار استراليّ
British pound	*junayh Istarliiniyy*	جنيه استرليني
Algerian dinar	*dinar Jazaa'iriy*	دينار جزائري
Tunisian dinar	*dinar Tunusiy*	دينار تونسي
Moroccan dirham	*dirham Maghribiy*	درهم مغربي
Lebanese pound	*lirah Lubnaniy-yah*	ليرة لبنانية
Muritannian ougiya	*'uoqiyah Muritaaniyah*	اوقية موريتانية
Lybian dinar	*dinaar Liibiy*	دينار ليبي
Sudanese pound	*junaih Sudaaniy*	جنيه سوداني
Omni riyal	*riyaal `Umaani*	ريال عماني
Kuwaiti dinar	*dinaar Kuwaytii*	دينار كويتي
Bahraini dinar	*dinaar Bahriiniy*	دينار بحريني
Iraqi dinar	*dinaar `Iraaqii*	دينارعراقي
Yemeni riyal	*riyaal Yamanii*	ريال يمني

Somali shilling	*shilin Somaali*	شلن صومالي
Djiboutian franc	*frank Jiibuutii*	فرنك جيبوتي
Comorian franc	*frank Qamarii*	فرنك قمري
Egyptian pound	*junayh Masriy*	جنيه مصري
Jordanian dinar	*dinaar Urduniy*	دينار أردني
Saudi riyal	*riyaal Sa`udii*	ريال سعودي
Syrian lira	*lairah Suuriy-yah*	ليرة سورية
UAE dirham	*dirham Imaraatii*	درهم إماراتي
U.S. dollar	*dulaar 'Amriikiyy*	دولار أمريكي
euro	*Uruu*	يورو/أورو
Singapore dollar	*duullaar Sanghafourii*	دولار سنغافوري
New Zealand dollar	*duullaar New Zelandii*	دولار نيوزيلندي
Canadian dollar	*duullaar Kanaadii*	دولار كندا
exchange	*tasriif `umlah*	تصريف عملة
traveler's check	*shiik siyaahii*	شيك سياحي
credit card	*bitaqah masrafiy-yah/ bitaaqatu i'timaan*	بطاقة مصرفية/ بطاقة ائتمان
prepaid card	*bitaaqah musbaqatud-daf'*	بطاقة مسبقة الدفع
debit card	*bitaaqatus-sahb*	بطاقة السحب
American Express	*Amariikan Eksbriis*	أمريكان إكسبريس
Mastercard	*Master caard*	ماستر كارد
Visa	*Fiizaa caard*	فيزا كارد
cash	*naqdan*	نقداً
expensive	*ghaalin*	غال
(commonly used as ***ghaalii***		غاليٍ)
cheap	*rakhiis*	

price (of the currency)	***si'r al 'umlah***	سعر العملة
bank	***masraf/bank***	مصرف/بنك
banks	***bunuuk***	بنوك
check	***shiik***	شيك
checks	***shiikaat***	شيكات
account	***hisaab***	حساب
business account	***hisaab jaarii***	حساب جاري
accounts	***hisaabaat***	حسابات
change (currency)	***taghyiir (al `umlah)***	تصريف (العملة)
foreign currency	***`umlah ajnabiy-yah***	عملة أجنبية
How many? (counting items)	***Kam?***	كم؟
How much? (asking the price)	***Bikam?***	بكم؟
budget	***miizaaniyyah***	ميزانية

What is the exchange rate for the U.S. dollar today?
Maa huwa si`r sarf addulaar al'amriikiyy alyawm?
ما هو سعر صرف الدولار الأمريكي اليوم؟

How much are these in local currency?
Kam haadhal-mablagh bil-`umlah almahalliyahh?
كم هذا المبلغ بالعملة المحلية؟

Please change 100 U.S. dollars into UAE dirham.
Momkin an tuhawwil mi'at dulaar amriikiyy `ilaa dirham imaaraatiyy?
ممكن أن تحول مئة درهم أمريكي إلى درهم إماراتي؟

Do you have change for 20 dinar?
`Indak fakkat `i<u>sh</u>riin diinaar? عندك فكة عشرين دينار؟

My budget is 3,000 riyals.
Miizaaniyyatii <u>th</u>alaa<u>th</u>at aalaaf riyaal.
ميزانيتي ثلاثة آلاف ريال.

This is a little expensive.
Haa<u>dh</u>aa <u>gh</u>alin qaliilan. هذا غالٍ قليلاً.

Could you give me a cheaper rate?
Mumkin an tu`<u>t</u>iinii si`r af<u>d</u>al?
ممكن أن تعطيني سعرأفضل؟

What is the currency of the country?
Maa hiyaa 'umlatul-balad? ما هي عملة البلد؟

Where can I find a bank? *Ayna al bank?* أين البنك؟

Are there any foreign banks here?
Hal yuujad bunuuk ajnabiyah hunaa?
هل يوجد بنوك أجنبية هنا؟

I would like to make a wire transfer.
'Uriidu an 'u<u>h</u>awil an-nquud iliktruniyan.
أريد أن أحول النقود إلكترونياً.

I would like to withdraw foreign money.
'Uriidu an as-<u>h</u>ab `umlah ajnabiyah.
أريد أن أسحب عملة أجنبية.

Is there a bank in this hotel?

Hal yuujad masrif/bank fii haadhaa al funduq?

هل يوجد مصرف/بنك في هذا الفندق؟

Is there an ATM machine?

Hal yuujad saraaf aaliy? هل يوجد صراف آلي؟

I would like to talk with the bank director/manager.

'Uriidu an atakallam ma` mudiir al bank.

أريد أن أتكلم مع مدير البنك.

The rates are very very expensive/cheap!

As`aar al`umlah ghaliyah/rakhiisah jiddan!

أسعار العملة غالية/رخيصة جداً!

Paying Bills

KEY WORDS AND EXPRESSIONS

bill	*faatuurah/hisaab*	فاتورة/حساب
receipt	*wasl*	وصل
cash	*naqdan*	نقداً
credit card	*bitaaqah i'timaan*	بطاقة ائتمان
How much?	*Kam/Bikam?*	كم/بكم؟
electricity bill	*faatuuatul-kahrabaa'*	فاتورة الكهرباء
gas bill	*fatuutrat al-ghaaz*	فاتورة الغاز
water bill	*faatuurat al-miyaahh*	فاتورة المياة
telephone bill	*faatuurat at-tilifuun/al haatif*	فاتورة التلفون/الهاتف
pay	*adfa`*	أدفع

payment *ad-daf`* الدفع
installment *taqsiit* تقسيط

A separate bill, please. *Hisaab munfasil law samaht.*
حساب منفصل لو سمحت.

How much is it altogether?
Kamil-hisaab bil kaamil? كم الحساب بالكامل؟

Do you accept credit cards? *Hal taqbal bitaaqaat i'timaan?*
هل تقبل بطاقات ائتمان؟

Can I pay by credit card?
Mumkin 'an 'adfa` bibitaaqatil-i'timaan?
ممكن أن أدفع ببطاقة الائتمان؟

A receipt, please. *Alwasl min fadlik.* الوصل من فضلك.

When is the bill due? *Mataa yajibu daf` al-faatuurah?*
متى يجب دفع الفاتورة؟

The bill is due monthly.
Todfa` al fatuurah shahriy-yan. تدفع الفاتورة شهريّاً.

The payment is past due. Please pay your bill.
Al faatuurah muta'akhhirah. arjuu ad-daf`.
الفاتورة متأخرة، أرجو الدفع.

You can pay the bill later.
Ymkinu daf` al faatuurah fiimaa ba`d.
يمكن دفع الفاتورة فيما بعد.

Are there utility bills? *Hal fawatiir al bayt madfu`ah?*
هل فواتير البيت مدفوعة؟

Could you help me pay the bill?
Hal mumkin musaa`idatii `alaa daf` al faatuurah?
هل ممكن مساعدتي في دفع الفاتورة؟

In a Restaurant

KEY WORDS AND EXPRESSIONS

food	*ta`am*	طعام
Arabian food	*ta`am `Arabii*	طعام عربي
Western food	*ta`am Gharbii*	طعام غربي
cafeteria	*maqsaf*	مقصف/كافتيريا
dining room	*ghurfatul-akl*	غرفة الأكل
coffee shop	*maqhaa*	مقهى
fast food	*wajbah sari`ah*	وجبة سريعة
food delivery	*tawsiil lilmanaazil*	توصيل للمنازل
menu	*qaaimatu ta`aam*	القائمة/قائمة طعام
meat	*lahm*	لحم
chicken	*dajaaj*	دجاج
fish	*samak*	سمك
seafood	*'aklaat bahriyyah*	أكلات بحرية
vegetables	*khudar/khudrawaat*	خضر/خضروات
hummus	*hummus*	حمص
fruits	*fawaakih*	فواكه
sugar	*sukkar*	سكر
salt	*milh*	ملح
pepper	*fulful aswad*	فلفل أسود
rice	*'aruzz*	أرز

soup	***hasaa`/shurbah***	حساء/شوربة
meal/meals	***wajbah/wajbaat***	وجبة/وجبات
main dish	***tabaq ra'iisii***	طبق رئيسي
side dish	***tabaq jaanibii***	طبق جانبي
dessert	***halwaa***	حلوى
ice cream	***muthallajaat***	مثلجات
(commonly used as it is in English)		
drink (n.)	***mashruub***	مشروب
water	***maa'***	ماء
boiling water	***maa' maghliyy***	ماء مغليّ
cold water	***maa' baarid***	ماء بارد
tea	***shay***	شاي
iced tea	***shay muthallaj***	شاي مثلج
coffee	***qahwah***	قهوة
black coffee	***qahwah saadah***	قهوة سادة
coffee without sugar	***qahwah murrah***	قهوة مرّة
coffee with sugar	***qahwah hulwah***	قهوة حلوة
coffee with milk	***qahwah bil-haliib***	قهوة بالحليب
milk	***haliib***	حليب
juice	***`asiir***	عصير
orange juice	***`asiir burtuqaal***	عصير برتقال
lemon juice	***`asiir laymuun***	عصير ليمون
apple juice	***`asiir tuffah***	عصير تفاح
strawberry juice	***`asiir farawla***	عصيرفرولة
banana juice	***`asiir mawz***	عصير موز
mineral water	***miyaah ma`daniyyah***	مياه معدنية
soft drink	***mashruub ghaaziyy***	مشروب غازي
table	***taawilah***	طاولة

knife	*sikkiin*	سكين
fork	*shawwkah*	شوكة
spoon	*mil`aqah*	ملعقة
plate	*sahn*	صحن
toothpick	*minkashat asnaan*	منكشة أسنان
napkin	*mindiil*	منديل
tray	*siiniyyah*	صينية
soap	*saabuun*	صابون
hot	*haarr/sukhn*	حار/سخن
cold	*baarid*	بارد
warm	*daafi'*	دافئ
delicious	*ladhiidh*	لذيذ
(common in Syria, Lebanon, Palestine and Jordan)		
not delicious	*ghayr ladhiidh*	غير لذيذ
sweet	*hulw*	حلو
salty	*maalih*	مالح
restaurant	*mat`am*	مطعم
restaurants	*mataa`im*	مطاعم
big	*kabiir*	كبير
big/big [fem.]	*kabiirah*	كبيرة
small	*saghiir*	صغير
small [fem.]	*saghiirah*	صغيرة
eat (v.)	*akala*	أكل
hungry	*jaa'i`/jaw`aan*	جائع/جوعان
hungry [fem.]	*jaa'i`ah/jaw`aanah*	جائعة/جوعانة
not hungry	*lastuu jaa'i`an*	لست جائعاً
not hungry [fem.]	*lastu jaa'i`ah*	لست جائعة
full	*shab`aan*	شبعان
full [fem.]	*shab`aanah*	شبعانة
thirst/thirsty	*`atshaan*	عطشان

thirst/thirsty [fem.]	*`atshaanah*	عطشانة
fine cuisine	*tabkh faakher*	طبخ فاخر
drink (v.)	*sharaba*	شرب
beverage	*mashruub*	مشروب
beverages	*mashruubaat*	مشروبات
warm	*daafi'*	دافئ
grilled	*mashwii*	مشوي
fried	*maqlii*	مقلي
steamed	*'alaa al-bukhaar*	على البخار
baked	*makhbuuz/* *matbuukh fil-furn*	مخبوز / مطبوخ في الفرن
chair	*kursii*	كرسي
chairs	*karaasii*	كراسي
waiter	*an-naadil*	النادل

I am hungry.

[MALE, COLLOQUIAL] *Ana jaa'i`.* أنا جائع.

[FEMALE, COLLOQUIAL] *Ana jaa'i`ah. ana jaw'aanah`.*
أنا جائعة. أنا جوعانة

Do you have an English menu?

Hal `indaka qaa'imat ta`aam bil injliiziyyah?
هل عندك قائمة طعام بالإنجليزية؟

What do you want to eat?

[MALE] *Maadha turiidu an ta'kul?*
ماذا تريد أن تأكل؟

[FEMALE] *Maadha turiidiin an ta'kuli?*
ماذا تريدين أن تأكلي؟

I am hungry. Ana jaa'i`ah.
Let's go out and eat something. Falnadh-hab lina'kula shay'an.
I like Middle Eastern food. 'Uhibuu an aakula ta`aam arabiyy.
What do you want to eat? Maadhaa turiidina an ta'kulii?
A table for two, please. Taawilah li shakhsayn law samaht.
This way, please. Tafadaluu ma`i.
Do you have an English menu? Hal `indakum qaa'imat ta`aam bil injliiziyyah?
Please bring us couscous with chicken and vegetables. 'Arjuu an tuhdira lanaa couscous bidajaaj wal khudrawaat.
Is that enough? Hal shabi'tii?
That is enough. Haadhaa kaafin.
It's on me. 'Anaa s'adfa`.

What time do you eat?

[MALE] ***Mataa ta'kul?*** متى تأكل؟

[FEMALE] ***Mataa ta'kuliin?***

متى تأكلين

Let's go out and eat something.

Falnadh-hab lina'kula shay'an. فلنذهب لنأكل شيئاً.

I like Arabian food.

'Uhibbut-ta`aam al`arabiyy. أحب الطعام العربيّ.

A table for two, please.

Taawilah li-shakhsayn law samaht.

طاولة لشخصين لو سمحت.

A menu, please. ***Qaa'imat atta`aam law samaht.***

قائمة الطعام لو سمحت.

What is this meal called?

Masmu haadhihil-wajbah? ما اسم هذه الوجبة؟

Please bring me....

[MALE] ***'Arjuu an tuhdira lii....*** أرجو أن تحضر لي....

[FEMALE] ***'Arjuu an tuhdirii lii....*** أرجو أن تحضري لي....

I would like to eat... ***'Awaddu/'uhibbu an 'aakula....***

أود/أحب أن آكل....

More salt and pepper please.

Almaziid minal milh wal-fulful al aswad law samaht.

المزيد من الملح و الفلفل الأسود لو سمحت.

Is that enough? *Hal haadhaa yakfii?* هل هذا يكفي؟

Please give me a little more.

'Arjuu an tu`tiinii akthar qaliilan.

أرجو أن تعطيني أكثر قليلاً.

That is enough. *Haadhaa kaafin.* هذا كافٍ.

That is too much. *Haadhaa kathiir.* هذا كثير.

I cannot eat all of this.

Laa 'astatii`u an 'aakula kulla haadhaa.

لا أستطيع أن آكل كل هذا.

Thanks for the delicious meal.

Shukran `alal-wajbah alladhiidhah.

شكراً على الوجبة اللذيذة.

I am thirsty.

[MALE] *Anaa `atshaan.* أنا عطشان.

[FEMALE] *Anaa `atshaanah.* أنا عطشانة.

What do you want to drink?

[MALE] *Maadhaa turiidu an tashrab?*

ماذا تريد أن تشرب؟

[FEMALE] *Maadhaa turiidiina an tashrabii?*

ماذا تريدين أن تشربي؟

I will have coffee, please.

Sa'aakhudhu qahwah law samaht.

سآخذ قهوة لو سمحت.

I will have black coffee, please.
Sa'aakhudhu qahwah saadah law samaht.
سآخذ قهوة سادة لو سمحت.

More coffee, please. *Almaziid minal-qahwah law samaht.*
المزيد من القهوة لو سمحت.

I will have tea with milk, please.
Sa'aakhudhu shaay ma`a haliib law samaht.
سآخذ شاي مع حليب لو سمحت.

Tea with lemon, please. *Shaay ma` laymuun law samaht.*
شاي مع ليمون لو سمحت.

A glass of milk, please. *Kuuba haliib, law samaht.*
كوب حليب، لو سمحت.

A bottle of mineral water, please.
Qaaruurat miyaah ma`daniyyah, law samaht.
قارورة مياه معدنيّة لو سمحت.

Yes, please. *na`am, min fadlik.* نعم، من فضلك.

No, thank you. *laa, shukran.* لا، شكراً.

The bill, please. *Alfaatuurah min fadlik.* الفاتورة من فضلك.
Alhisaab min fadlik. الحساب من فضلك.

Paying the bills

It's expected that the person who extends the invitation foots the bill. Refrain from suggesting to split the bill at the restaurant. If you feel you must reciprocate your host's treat, try doing something in return, e.g., giving the host a treat in return. Never do the accounting openly at the table.

Alcohol In Middle Eastern Countries

Muslims are forbidden from consuming both pork and alcohol, and as such these products are difficult to find in many Middle Eastern countries, and illegal in others.

At the Cafe

Traditional cafes in the Arab world are mainly open for men only. Hot and cold beverages are served in these types of coffee shops, as well as sweets and maybe ice cream, but definitely not alcohol. In countries like Egypt, Lebanon, Syria and Jordan cafés are specialized in ***shisha***, the Arabic name for ***nargila/hookah*** served along with tea and Turkish coffee.

KEY WORDS AND EXPRESSIONS

café/coffee shop	***maqhaa***	مقهى
beverage	***mashruub***	مشروب
beverages	***mashrubaat***	مشروبات
cold beverages	***mashruubaat baaridah***	مشروبات باردة
hot beverages	***mashruubaat saakhinah***	مشروبات ساخنة
ice cream	***muthallajaat/ buzah***	مثلجات/بوظة

coffee	*qahwah*	قهوة
black coffee	*qahwaa saadaa*	قهوة سادة
milk	*haliib/laban*	حليب/لبن
coffee with milk	*qahwa bi-haliib*	قهوة بحليب
cappuccino	*kaabutshinuu*	كابتشينو
hot	*saakhin*	ساخن
cold	*baarid*	بارد
sugar	*sukkar*	سكر
cup	*finjaan*	فنجان
glass	*ka's*	كأس
juice	*`asiir*	عصير
orange juice	*`asiir burtuqaal*	عصير برتقال
lemon juice	*`asiir laymuun*	عصير ليمون
strawberry juice	*`asiir faraawlah*	عصير فراولة
grape juice	*`asiir `inab*	عصير عنب
banana juice	*`asiir mawz*	عصير موز
apple juice	*`asiir tuffah*	عصير تفاح
sweet	*halawiy-yaat*	حلويات
plate	*sahn*	صحن
spoon	*mil`aqah*	ملعقة
napkin	*mindiil*	منديل
table	*taawilah*	طاولة
chair	*kursiy*	كرسي
chair/chairs	*karaasii*	كراسي
waiter	*an-naadil*	النادل
not allowed to smoke	*ghayr masmouh bit-tadkhiin*	غير مسموح بالتدخين
water	*maa'*	ماء
tea	*shay*	شاي
order (n.)	*talab*	طلب

order (v.)	*talaba*	طلب
tray	*siniyah*	صينية
people	*ashkhaas/afraad*	أشخاص/أفراد

Popular Pastries in the Middle East

Besbuusah بسبوسه
Traditional Middle Eastern sweet cake with cooked semolina or farina soaked in syrup. Popular additions include coconut.

Kunafah كنافة
A traditional Palestinian dessert made with cheese pastry in syrup, usually found in Levant, Egypt, Turkey and Greece.

Fatayer فطاير
A meat pie that is eaten in Iraq, Syria, and other Arab countries. Alternate stuffings include spinach or cheese.

Qatayef قطايف
A sweet dumpling filled with cream or nuts served during Ramadaan.

Tea and coffee with some *besbuusah*, please.
Shaay wa qahwa ma`a basbuusa, min fadlik.
شاي و قهوة مع بسبوسة من فضلك.

Coffee with no milk. *Qahwa biduun haliib/laban.*
قهوة بدون حليب/لبن.

One coffee and two pieces of *kataif* (sweet).
Qahawa wa qit`atain qatayef. قهوة و قطعتين قطايف.

A glass of orange juice, please.
Kuub `asiir burtuqaal min fadlik.
كوب عصير برتقال من فضلك.

Two cups of tea. *Ka'sain shay.* كأسين شاي.

A cup of coffee (with no sugar) and one with milk.
Finjaan qahwaa saadah wa finjaan qahwa bi-hlaiib.
فنجان قهوة سادة و فنجان قهوة بحليب.

Sugar please. *Assukkar min fadlik.* السكر من فضلك.

Coffee for five people at the table outside.
Qahwah li-khamsat afraad `alaa at-taawila fil-khaarij.
قهوة لخمسة أفراد على الطاولة في الخارج.

Green tea with mint. *Shay akhdar bina`na` min fadlik.*
شاي أخضر بنعناع من فضلك.

One strawberry juice, please.
Min fadlik `asiir farawlah. من فضلك عصير فراولة.

Let's have coffee at the neighborhood coffee shop.
Ta`aalaa nashrabu qahwa fii maqhaa al-haarah.
تعال نشرب قهوة في مقهى الحارة.

Is there a traditional coffee shop in this neighborhood?

Hal yuujad maqhaa 'arabiy fi haa<u>dh</u>aal-<u>h</u>ay?

هل يوجد مقهى عربي في هذا الحي؟

Where is the coffee shop, please?

Aynal-maqhaa min fa<u>d</u>lik? أين المقهى من فضلك؟

I'll see you at the café this evening, God willing.

Sa-araaka fil maqhaa haa<u>dh</u>al-masaa', inshaa' Allah.

سأراك في المقهى هذا المساء، إن شاء لله.

I like coffee but prefer tea.

'U<u>h</u>ibbu al qahwa wa laakin 'ufa<u>dd</u>ilu a<u>sh</u>-<u>sh</u>aay.

أحب القهوة و لكن أفضل الشاي.

Is this Arabic/Turkish coffee?

Hal haa<u>dh</u>ihii qahwah 'arabiy-yah?

هل هذه قهوة عربية؟

At the Hotel

KEY WORDS AND EXPRESSIONS

hotel	*funduq*	فندق
reservations	*al-<u>h</u>ujuuzaat*	الحجوزات
room	*<u>gh</u>urfah*	غرفة
suite	*janaa<u>h</u>*	جناح
pool	*masba<u>h</u>*	مسبح
swimming pool	*<u>h</u>ammaam sibaa<u>h</u>ah*	حمام سباحة
reception	*'istiqbaal*	استقبال

receptionist	*mu'azzaf al'istiqbaal*	موظف الاستقبال
receptionist	*mu'azzahat-al'istiqbaal*	موظفة الاستقبال
lobby	*luby/rudhah*	لوبي/ردهة
elevator	*mas`ad kahrabaa'iy/ asansiir* [COLLOQUIAL]	مصعد كهربائي/ اسنسير
escalator	*daraj kahrabaa'iy*	درج كهربايئ
stairs	*daraj*	درج
vacation	*ijaazah*	إجازة
single	*mufrad*	مفرد
double	*muzdawaj*	مزدوج
bed	*sariir*	سرير
large	*kabiir*	كبير
small	*saghiir*	صغير
clean	*naziif*	نظيف
cleaner	*munazzif*	منظف
maid	*`aamilatu annazaafah*	عاملة النظافة
room number	*raqm al-ghurfah*	رقم الغرفة
key	*muftaah*	مفتاح
air conditioning	*takyiif hawaa'*	تكييف هواء
blanket	*ghitaa'*	غطاء
pillow	*wisaadah/makhad-dah*	وسادة/مخدة
laundry	*ghasiil*	غسيل
tip [COLLOQUIAL]	*baqshiish*	بقشيش
emergency exit	*makhraj al-tawari'*	مخرج الطوارئ
exit	*makhraj*	مخرج
bathroom	*hammam*	حمام
bedsheets	*firaash*	فراش
telephone	*al-haatif*	الهاتف
first floor	*ad-dawr al-awwal*	الدور الأول

second floor	*ad-dawr ath-thaanii*	الدور الثاني
upper floor	*ad-dawr al-`ulwii*	الدور العلوي
lower floor	*ad-dawr as-suflii*	الدور السفلي
shower [COLLOQUIAL]	*al-mirash/dush*	المرش/دش
soap	*saabuun*	صابون
towel	*mishafah*	منشفة
bath tub	*hawd al-istihmaam*	حوض الاستحمام
there is	*yuujed*	يوجد
there isn't	*laa yuujed*	لا يوجد
double beds	*sariir zawjii*	سرير زوجي
cold	*baarid*	بارد
stars (rating)	*nujuum*	نجوم
reserved	*mahjuuzah* (f)	محجوزة
lock	*qifl*	قفل
rate	*si`r*	سعر
closed	*mughlaq*	مغلق
opened	*maftuuh*	مفتوح
duration	*mud-dah*	مدة
heat	*tadfi'ah*	تدفئة
breakfast	*iftaar/futuur as-sabaah*	إفطار/فطور الصباح
balcony	*shurfah*	شرفة

My name is …; I have a reservation.
Ismii …; `indii hajz. اسمي ... عندي حجز.

Here's my booking confirmation. *Tafaddal raqam al-hajz.*
تفضل رقم الحجز.

My name is Cheryl; I have a reservation.
Ismii Cheryl; ladayya hajz fi funduqikum.
Here is my booking confirmation.
Tafadali, raqam al hajz.
Please pass me your passport too.
Min fadliki, a'tini jawaaz as-safar.
NO SMOKING
Thank you. Does the room have Wi-Fi?
Shukran. Hal yuujadu Wi-Fi *fi-ilghurfa?*
Yes, all our rooms have complimentary Wi-Fi.
N'am, al Wi-Fi *majjanii fi kul alghuraf.*
What time does the restaurant open?
Fii ayi saa'a yaftahul almat`am?
It opens at 6 a.m.
As-saa'a as-saadisah sabaahan.

Do you have a vacant room?

Hal `indaka ghurfah shaaghirah? هل عندك غرفة شاغرة؟

Do you have a vacant room for one person?

Hal `indaka ghurfah shaaghirah li-shakhsin waahid? هل عندك غرفة شاغرة لشخصٍ واحد؟

Do you have a vacant room for two people?

Hal `indaka ghurfah shaaghirah lishakhsayn?
هل عندك غرفة شاغرة لشخصين؟

Do you have a room with a balcony?

Hal `indaka ghurfah bi-shurfah?
هل عندك غرفة بشرفة؟

Do you have a room with Internet?

Hal `indaka ghurfa fiiha Internet?
هل عندك غرفة فيها انترنت؟

Do you have a room with Wi-Fi?

Hal `indaka ghurfa fiiha Wi-Fi?
هل عندك غرفة فيها وايفاي؟

Is the Wi-Fi complimentary?

Hal al way fay majjanii? هل الواي فاي مجاني

OR *Hal al khidmah tashmul al way fay?*
هل الخدمة تشمل الواي فاي؟

What's my room number? ***Maa raqamu ghurfatii?***
ما رقم غرفتي؟

Do you have a single room?
Hal `indaka ghurfah bisariir mufrad?
هل عندك غرفة بسرير مفرد؟

Do you have a double room?
Hal `indaka ghurfah bisariir muzdawaj?
هل عندك غرفة بسرير مزدوج؟

Do you have a larger room?
Hal `indaka ghurfah akbar? هل عندك غرفة أكبر؟

I want a room for two nights.
'Uriidu ghurfah lilaylatayn. أريد غرفة لليلتين؟

I want a room with a sea view.
'Uriidu ghurfatan tutillu `alal-bahr.
أريد غرفة تطلّ على البحر.

What is the rate for this room?
Kam ujratu haadhihil-ghurfah? كم أجرة هذه الغرفة؟

What time does the restaurant open?
Mataa yaftahul-mat`am? متى يفتح المطعم؟

Please send someone to clean my room.
'Arsil man yunazziful-ghurfah min fadlik.
أرسل من ينظف الغرفة من فضلك.

What time is breakfast? *Matai-iftaar?* متى الإفطار؟

Please wake me up at 7 a.m.
'Arjuu an tuuqizanii fis-saa`atis-saabi`ah sabaahan.
أرجو أن توقظني في الساعة السابعة صباحا.

Is there an English newspaper?
Hal hunaaka jariidah bil-injliiziyyah?
هل هناك جريدة بالإنجليزيّة؟

Where can I get a map?
Min ayna yumkin an ahsula `alaa khariitah?
من أين يمكن أن أحصل على خريطة؟

I have lost my room key. *Laqad ada`tu miftaaha ghurfatii.*
لقد أضعت مفتاح غرفتي.

Are there any messages for me?
Hal hunaaka ayyatu rasaa'il lii?
هل هناك أيّة رسائل لي؟

I have some laundry. *`Indii ba`dul-ghasiil.*
عندي بعض الغسيل.

I need another blanket.
'Ahtaaju `ilaa ghitaa'in aakhar. أحتاج إلى غطاء آخر.

When will the laundry be ready?
Mataa sayakuunul-ghasiil jaahizan?
متى سيكون الغسيل جاهزاً؟

I would like to extend my reservation.

'Awaddu an `umaddida hajzii. أودّ أن أمدّد حجزي.

I would like to stay for two more days.

'Awaddu an abqaa li yawmayyn `idaafiyyayn.
أودّ أن أبقى ليومين إضافيين.

How far is it from the hotel?

Kam huwa ba`iid minal-funduq? كم هو بعيد من الفندق؟

Can I walk there from the hotel?

Hal yumkinunii an 'amshii `ilaa hunaak minal-funduq? هل يمكنني أن أمشي إلى هناك من الفندق؟

Please call a taxi for me.

'Utlub sayyarata `ujrah min fadlik.
اطلب سيارة أجرة من فضلك.

What time is checkout? *Mataa yajibu an `ughaadir?*
متى يجب أن أغادر؟

Going Somewhere

KEY WORDS AND EXPRESSIONS

cinema	*sinamaa*	سينما
restaurant	*mat`am*	مطعم
theater	*masrah*	مسرح
bank	*bank*	بنك
picnic	*rihlah*	رحلة
beach	*shaat'i al-bahr*	شاطئ البحر

café	*al-maqhaa*	المقهى
museum	*al-mathaf*	المتحف
library	*al-maktabah*	المكتبة
mall	*al-muul*	المول
shopping center	*at-tajammu` at-tijaari*	التجمع التجاري
bookstore	*al-maktabah*	المكتبة
park	*al-hadiiqah/albark*	الحديقة/البارك
north	*shamaal*	شمال
south	*januub*	جنوب
east	*sharq*	شرق
west	*gharb*	غرب
right	*yamiin*	يمين
left	*yasaar*	يسار
in front of	*'amaam*	أمام
behind	*khalf*	خلف
beside	*bi-jaanib*	بجانب
near	*qariib*	قريب
far	*ba`iid*	بعيد
above	*fawq*	فوق
under	*taht*	تحت

I want to go and see a movie.
'Uriidu an ushaahid film. أريد أن أشاهد فيلم.

Oh! That's a good idea! *Fikrah jayyidah!* فكرة جيدة!

Would you like to go with me?
Hal tawaddu an ta'tii ma`ii? هل تودّ أن تأتي معي؟

I want to go and see a movie. ***'Uriidu an ushaahid fiilm.***
Oh! That's a good idea! ***Fikrah jayyidah!***
Would you like to go with me? ***Hal tawaddu an ta'tii ma`ii?***
I am afraid I can't this evening. ***'Akhshaa annanii laa astatii` haadhal masaa'.***
How about tomorrow? ***Ghadan?***
Yes, that would be good. ***Na`am, ghadan, inshaa'Allah.***

I'm afraid I can't this evening.
'Akhshaa annanii laa astatii` haadhal-masaa'
أخشى أنني لا أستطيع هذا المساء.

How about tomorrow? [COLLOQUIAL] *Ghadan?* غداً؟

Yes, that would be good.
Na`am, haadhihi fikratun jayyidah.
نعم، هذه فكرة جيدة.

I'm sorry. I've an appointment.
'Anaa aasif, `indii maw`id. أنا أسف، عندي موعد.

Let's go for a walk.
Fal-natamash-shaa qaliilan. فلنتمشى قليلاً.

Let's go to a falafel restaurant.
Fal-nadh-hab 'ilaa mat`am falaafil.
فلنذهب إلى مطعم فلافل.

Is it nearby? *Hal huwa qariib?* هل هو قريب؟

Can we walk there? *Mumkin 'an namshii 'ilaa hunaak?*
ممكن أن نمشي إلى هناك؟

No, let's take a taxi. *Laa, lina'khudh sayyaarata 'ujrah.*
لا، لنأخذ سيارة أجرة.

In a Taxi

KEY WORDS AND EXPRESSIONS

taxi	*sayyaarat 'ujrah*	طاكسي سيارة أجرة
stop/stand (n.)	*mawqif*	موقف
fare	*'ujrah*	أجرة
gauge/meter	*a`ddaad*	عداد
driver	*saa`iq*	سائق
left (direction)	*yasaar*	يسار
right (direction)	*yamiin*	يمين
straight [COLLOQUIAL]	*'ilal-`amaam*	إلى الأمام
intersection	*taqaa<u>t</u>u`*	تقاطع
corner	*rukn*	ركن
address	*`unwaan*	عنوان
road	*<u>t</u>ariq*	طريق
street	*<u>sh</u>aari`*	شارع
How much?	*Bikam?*	بكم؟
distance	*al masafah*	المسافة
far/far [fem.]	*ba`iid/ba'iidah*	بعيد/بعيدة
close/close [fem.]	*qariib/qariibah*	قريب/ قريبة
(the) **city**	*al-madinah*	المدينة
(the) **university**	*al-jami`ah*	الجامعة
(the) **market**	*as-souq*	السوق
(the) **café**	*al-maqhaa*	المقهى
(the) **airport**	*al-ma<u>t</u>aar*	المطار
(the) **hotel**	*al-funduq*	الفندق
station	*ma<u>h</u>a<u>t</u>tah*	محطة
(the) **train**	*al-qi<u>t</u>aar*	القطار
bus	*<u>h</u>aafilah/baa<u>s</u>*	حافلة/باص

currency	*`umlah*	عملة
appointment	*maw`id*	موعد
arrival	*wusuul*	وصول
(the) **door**	*al-baab*	الباب
(the) **front**	*al-amaamiy*	الأمامي
(the) **back**	*al-khalfiy*	الخلفي
(the) **luggage**	*al-amti`ah*	الأمتعة
seat	*kursiy*	كرسي
suitcases	*haqaa'ib*	حقائب
slow	*but'*	بطء
speed	*sur`ah*	سرعة
there	*hunaak*	هناك
here	*hunaa*	هنا
after	*ba`d*	بعد
before	*qabl*	قبل
from	*min*	من
to	*ilaa*	إلى
wait	*intazir*	انتظر
I want to	*'uriid*	أريد
North	*Shamaal/Shimaal*	شمال
West	*Gharb*	غرب
East	*Sharq*	شرق
South	*Januub*	جنوب
expensive	*ghaalii*	غالي
cheap	*rakhiis*	رخيص

I want to go to the airport, please.

Uriidu an adh-haba 'ilaa al-mataar law samaht.

أريد أن أذهب إلى المطار لو سمحت.

I want to go to the train station, please.

Uriidu an adh-haba ilaa mhatat al-qitaar law samaht.

أريد أن أذهب إلى محطة القطار لو سمحت.

I want to go to the bus station, please.

Uriidu an adh-haba ilaa mahatat al-baasaat/alhaafilaat law samaht.

أريد أن أذهب إلى محطة الباصات/الحافلات لو سمحت.

I am in a hurry. *Anaa musta`jil.* أنا مستعجل.

How long does it take to reach...?

Kam minal-waqt nahtaaj linasila 'ilaa...?

كم من الوقت نحتاج لنصل إلى...؟

Please come and pick me up at 9:00 a.m.

Arjuu an ta'tiya lita'khudhanii fis-saa`atit-taasi`ah sabaahan. أرجو أن تأتي لتأخذني في الساعة التاسعة صباحاً

Take me to this address, please.

Khudhnii 'ilaa haadhal-`unwaan law samaht.

خذني إلى هذا العنوان لو سمحت.

Wait for me.

Intazirnii min fadlik. انتظرني من فضلك

How much is the fare, please?

Kamil-'ujrah law samaht? كم الأجرة لو سمحت؟

The fare is very expensive.

Al-'ujrah ghaaliyah jidan. الأجرة غالية جداً.

I want to go to the Ibis hotel, please. *Uriidu an a__dh__-haba ilaa funduq ibis law sama__h__t.*
It's 50 dirhams. ***Kh**amsuna dirham.*
How much is the fare, please? *Bikam al' ujrah, min fa__d__lek?*
Okay, let's go. *Jay-yid. lina__dh__-hab.*
Do you take credit cards? *Hal ta'__kh__u__dh__ bi__t__a-aqat ali'itimaan?*
Sorry, cash only. *Aasif. Naqdan/ cash faqa__t__.*
Okay. Here you go. I need help with my luggage. ***T**ayeb, tafa__d__al. A__h__taaj musa`adah li__h__aml al-amti`ah.*
Thanks a lot! ***Sh**ukran jaziilan!*

Please go straight ahead.
`Ala tuul law samaht. على طول لو سمحت.

Please turn right here.
'Ilal-yamiin law samaht. إلى اليمين لو سمحت.

Please turn left at the next street.
`Alal-yasaar minash-shaari` at-taalii.
على اليسار من الشارع التالي.

Please slow down. *Bibut' law samaht.* ببطء لو سمحت.

Do you take foreign currency?
Hal taqbal `umlah ajnabiyah? هل تقبل عملة أجنبية؟

Do you take credit cards?
Hal taqbal bitaaqat ali'itimaan? هل تقبل بطاقة الائتمان؟

Do you take e-payment? *Hal taqbal addaf` al electroniy?*
هل تقبل الدفع الالكتروني؟

I need help with my luggage.
Ahtaaj musa`adah lihaml al-amti`ah.
أحتاج مساعدة لحمل الأمتعة.

Please come back in an hour.
Min fadlik irje` ba`d saa`ah. من فضلك ارجع بعد ساعة.

I need a taxi from ... to ...
...Ahtaaj taaksii minas-saa`ah... 'ilaas-saa`ah...
...أحتاج تاكسي من الساعة... إلى الساعة...

Please stop. *Tawaqaf min fadlik.* توقف من فضلك.

I will be back in 5 minutes.
Sa'a`uudu ba`da khamsi daqaa'iq.
سأعود بعد خمس دقائق.

At the Station

KEY WORDS AND EXPRESSIONS

public transportation	*muwaasalaat `umuumiy-yah*	مواصلات عموميّة
bus stop/ stand	**haafilah/baas mawqif (al-baas)*	حافلة/باص موقف (الباص)

* ***haafilah*** is the proper word for "bus" but ***baas*** is so common that it can be used.

bus depot	*mujamma` al-baasaat*	مُجمَّع الباصات
driver	*saa'iq*	سائق
train	*qitaar*	قطار
train station	*mahatat qitaar*	محطة قطار
railway express	*sikak hadiidiyyah qitaar sari`*	سكك حديدية قطار سريع
steam train	*qitaar bukhaarii*	قطار بخاري
train ticket officer	*muwazzaf attadhaakir*	موظف التذاكر
ticket office	*maktab attadhaakir*	مكتب التذاكر
one-way ticket	*tadhkarat dhahaab*	تذكرة ذهاب
return ticket	*tadhkarat 'iyaab*	تذكرة إياب
schedule	*jadwal*	جدول
timetable	*jadwal `amal*	جدول عمل
get on	*yas`ad 'ilaa*	يصعد إلى
get off	*yanzil min*	ينزل من

Is there a bus stop nearby?

Hal yuujadu mawqifu baasaat qariibun min hunaa?

هل يوجد موقف باصات قريب من هنا؟

Where is the bus station?

'Ayna mahattat albaasat? أين محطة الباصات؟

How can I get to the bus station?

Kayfa yumkinunii 'an 'adh-haba `ilaa mahattatil-baas?

كيف يمكنني أن أذهب إلى محطة الباص؟

Which bus should I take to go to Hamidiyya Market?

'Ayyu baas yajibu 'an 'aakhudha li'adh-haba `ilaa souqil-hamiidiyyah?

أي باص يجب أن آخذ لأذهب إلى سوق الحميدية؟

What is the bus fare? *Kam 'ujratul-baas?* كم أجرة الباص؟

Do you have the bus schedule/timetable?

Hal ladayka jadwal `amal al-baasaat?

هل لديك جدول عمل الباصات؟

Where does the downtown bus leave from?

Min 'ayna yantaliq albaas almutawajjih 'ilaa markazil madiinah? من أين ينطلق الباص المتوجه إلى مركز المدينة؟

Is there a bus that goes to the airport?

Hal hunaaka baas yadh-habu 'ilal-mataar?

هل هناك باص يذهب إلى المطار؟

Where is the train station?

   'Ayna ma<u>h</u>a<u>tt</u>atil qi<u>t</u>aar?   أين محطة القطار؟

I want to go to Cairo by train.

   'Uriidu 'an 'a<u>dh</u>-haba 'laal-qahirah bil qi<u>t</u>aar.
أريد أن أذهب إلى القاهرة بالقطار.

Where should I get on the train that goes to...?

   Min 'ayna 'aa<u>kh</u>u<u>dh</u>ul-qi<u>t</u>aar mutawajjih 'ilaa ...?
من أين آخذ القطار المتوجه إلى...؟

How can I go to the train station?

   Kayfa a<u>dh</u>-habu `ilaa ma<u>h</u>a<u>tt</u>atil-qi<u>t</u>aar?
كيف أذهب إلى محطة القطار؟

Please take me to the train station.

   Arjuu 'an ta'<u>kh</u>u<u>dh</u>anii 'ilaa ma<u>h</u>a<u>tt</u>atil-qi<u>t</u>aar.
أرجو أن تأخذني إلى محطة القطار.

Where can I buy a ticket?

   Min 'ayna yumkinunii 'an 'a<u>sh</u>tarii ta<u>dh</u>karah?
من أين يمكنني أن أشتري تذكرة؟

How much is the train ticket?

   Bikam ta<u>dh</u>karatul-qi<u>t</u>aar?   بكم تذكرة القطار؟

Shopping

KEY WORDS AND EXPRESSIONS

shopping center/mall	*markaz tijaarii/ tasawwuq*	مركز تجاري/ تسوق
shopping centers/malls	*maraakiz tijaariyyah /tasawwuq*	مراكز تجارية/ تسوق
shop	*mahal/dukkaan*	محل/دكان
gift shop	*mahal hadaayaa*	محل هدايا
grocery	*baqqaalah*	بقالة
bookstore	*maktabah*	مكتبة
antiques	*tuhaf*	تحف
souvenirs	*tadhkaar*	تذكار
greeting cards	*bitaaqaat tahni'ah*	بطاقات تهنئة
poster	*mulsaq*	ملصق
book	*kitaab*	كتاب
clothes	*malaabis*	ملابس
jewelry	*mujawharaat*	مجوهرات
accessories	*kamaaliyyaat*	كماليات
toys	*'al`aab*	ألعاب
watches	*saa`aat*	ساعات
leather	*jild*	جلد
tourist map	*khariitat-suyyaah*	خريطة سياح
English-Arabic dictionary	*qaamuus injliiziyy `arabiyy*	قاموس إنجليزيّ عربيّ
birthday	*`iid miilaad*	عيد ميلاد
Christmas	*`iid al-miilaad al-majiid*	عيد الميلاد المجيد
wedding anniversary	*dhikraa zawaaj*	ذكرى زواج

Mother's Day	*'iidul-'umm*	عيد الأم
Father's Day	*'iidul-'ab*	عيد الأب
Valentine's Day	*'iidul-hub*	عيد الحب
how much	*bikam*	بكم
discount	*khasm/takhfiid*	خصم/تخفيض
expensive	*ghaalii*	غالي
cheap	*rakhiis*	رخيص
large/big	*kabiir/waasi`*	كبير/واسع
small	*saghiir*	صغير
tight	*dayyiq*	ضيق
buy	*shiraa'*	شراء
grocery	*biqaalah*	بقالة
vegetables	*khudrawaat*	خضروات
meat	*luhuum*	لحوم
clothing	*malaabis*	ملابس
home supplies	*haajiyaat manziliyyah*	حاجيات منزلية

I will buy... . *Sa'ashtarii... .* سأشتري... .

I want to buy... . *'Uriidu 'an 'ashtarii... .* أريد أن أشتري... .

I would like to buy it.
'Awaddu 'an 'ashtariih. أود أن اشتريته.

I bought it. *'Ishtaraytahu.* اشتريته.

I am not going to buy it. *Lan 'ashtariih.* لن أشتريه.

Did you buy it? *Hal-ish-taraytahu?* هل اشتريته؟

How much did you buy it for?
Bikamis<u>h</u>-taraytahu? بكم اشتريته؟

Who bought it? ***Manis<u>h</u> taraah?*** من اشتراه؟

What do you want to buy?
[MALE] ***Maa<u>dh</u>a turiid 'an tas<u>h</u>tarii?***
ماذا تريد أن تشتري؟
[FEMALE] ***Maa<u>dh</u>a turiidiina 'an tas<u>h</u>tarii?***
ماذا تريدين أن تشتري؟

Where did you buy that from?
[MALE] ***Min ayna-<u>sh</u> taaraytah?*** من أين اشتريته؟
[FEMALE] ***Min ayna-<u>sh</u> taaraytih?*** من أين اشتريته؟

What did you buy? ***Maa<u>dh</u>a<u>sh</u> tarayt?*** ماذا اشتريت؟

Is there a shopping center nearby?
Hal yuujadu markazu tasawwuqin qariib?
هل يوجد مركز تسوّق قريب؟

How much is this in U.S. dollars?
Bikam haa<u>dh</u>aa biddulaar al'amriikiyy?
بكم هذا بالدولار الأمريكيّ؟

I'm just browsing. ***'Ana 'atafarraj faqa<u>t</u>.*** أنا أتفرّج فقط.

I'd like a pair of shoes, please.
'Awaddu <u>sh</u>iraa'a zawj 'a<u>hdh</u>iyah law sama<u>h</u>t.
أودّ شراء زوج أحذية لو سمحت.

Is there a shopping center nearby? *Hal yuujadu markaz tasawwuq qariib?*
Yes, it's across the road. *N`am, huwa `alaa al jaanib al-aakhar minat tariiq.*
What are you looking for? *Maadhaa turiidiina an tashtari?*
I want to buy some clothes. *'Uriduu shiraa`a ba'd al malaabis.*
Hi, can I help you with anything? *Ahlan wa marhaba hal tahtajiin ayat musaa'adah?*
I am just browsing. *'Ana 'atafarraj faqat.*
I want that jacket. *'Urridu dhaalika mi`taf.*
How much is this? *Bikam haadhaa?*
It's 1,770 EGP. *Bi-alf wa sab`u mi'aa wa sab'uun dirham.*
This is very expensive. *Haadhaa ghaalin jiddan.*
Is the price negotiable? *Hal mumkin takhfiidh as-si`r?*
There's a 20 per cent discount. *Fiih takhfidh binisbat `ishriin bilm-i'ah.*
I'll take it. *S'aakhuduhu.*

I need some razor blades.
'A<u>h</u>taaju 'ilaa <u>sh</u>afraat. أحتاج إلى شفرات.

I need some sanitary napkins.
'A<u>h</u>taaju 'ilaa manaadiil. أحتاج إلى مناديل.

I'm looking for… . *'Ana 'ab<u>h</u>a<u>th</u>u `an… .* أنا أبحث عن… .

How much is this? *Bikam haa<u>dh</u>aa?* بكم هذا؟

I want that jacket.
'Uriidu <u>dh</u>aalikal mi`<u>t</u>af. أريد ذلك المعطف.

May I have a receipt?
Alwa<u>s</u>l law sama<u>h</u>t? الوصل لو سمحت؟

Do you accept Australian dollars?
Hal taqbalu dulaaraat 'usturaaliyyah?
هل تقبل دولارات أسترالية؟

I want to buy a present for my wife.
`Uriidu 'an 'a<u>sh</u>tarii hadiyyatan li zawjatii.
أريد أن أشتري هدية لزوجتي.

Please show me… *Ariiny min fa<u>d</u>lik…* أرني من فضلك…

May I see that… ? *Hal yumkinunii 'an 'araa <u>dh</u>aalik al…?*
هل يمكنني أن أرى ذلك ال… ؟

I want to buy it. *'Uriidu 'an 'a<u>sh</u>tariih.* أريد أن أشتريه.

What is the price, please?
Maa huwas si`r min fadlik? ما هو السعر من فضلك؟

How much does this cost?
Kam yukallifu haadhaa? كم يكلف هذا؟

Is the price negotiable? *Halis si`r qaabil littafaawud?*
هل السعر قابل للتقاوض؟

Are prices fixed here? *Hal al-as`aar thaabitah hunaa?*
هل الأسعار ثابتة هنا؟

This is very expensive.
Haadhaa ghaalin jiddan. هذا غالٍ جدّاً.

This is very cheap.
Haadhaa rakhiis jiddan. هذا رخيص جداً.

Locating Restrooms

KEY WORDS AND EXPRESSIONS

toilet	*hammam/mirhaad*	حمام/مرحاض
toilets	*hammamaat/ maraahid*	حمامات/ مراحض
Where?	*Ayna?*	أين؟
men	*rijaal*	رجال
women/ladies	*nisaa'/say-yidaat*	نساء/سيدات
water	*maa'/miyaah*	ماء/مياه
sink	*hawd*	حوض
faucet/tap	*hanafiah/sanbuur*	حنفية/صنبور

cold water	***maa' baarid***	ماء بارد
hot water	***maa' saakhen***	ماء ساخن
soap	***saabuun***	صابون
liquid soap	***saabuun saail***	صابون سائل
toilet paper	***waraq al hammaam***	ورق الحمام
men's toilet	***hammaam rijaal***	حمام رجال
women's toilet	***hammaam sayyidaat***	حمام سيدات
public toilet	***hammaam `umuumiyy***	حمام عموميّ
washroom	***maghaasil***	مغاسل
hand dryer	***mujafif al yad***	مجفف اليد

Is there a toilet here?

Hal yuujad hammaam hunaa? هل يوجد حمام هنا؟

Where is the toilet please?

Aynal hammaam min fadlik? أين الحمام من فضلك؟

Is there a public toilet nearby?

Hal yuujadu hammaam `umuumiyy qariib?

هل يوجد حمام عموميّ قريب؟

I need to go to the toilet.

'Ahtaaju an adh-haba ilal hammaam.

أحتاج أن أذهب إلى الحمام.

May I use the toilet please?

Mumkin an astakhdimal hammaam min fadlik?

ممكن أن أستخدم الحمام من فضلك؟

Where are the ladies' restrooms?

Ayna hammamu as-say-yidaat? أين حمام السيدات؟

Are these the men's restrooms?

Hal hadhaa huwa hammamur-rijaal?

هل هذا هو حمام الرجال؟

Are the restrooms far away?

Hal al ham-mamaat ba`iidah? هل الحمامات بعيدة؟

I'm looking for the men's room, please.

Min fadlik abhathu `an mirhaad ar-rijaal?

من فضلك، أبحث عن مرحاض للرجال؟

There are no public restrooms!

Laa yujaad maraahiid `umuumiy-yah!

لا يوجد حمامات عموميّة!

The public restrooms are next to the exit.

Al hammam al `umuumiy bijaanib al makhraj.

الحمام العموميّ بجانب المخرج.

The public restrooms are closed now.

Almaraahid al`umumiyah mughlaqah al aan.

المراحض العموميّة مغلقة الآن.

I will go to the closest men's restrooms.

Sa'adhhabu ilaa aqrab hammam lir-rijaal.

سأذهب إلى أقرب حمام للرجال.

There is no toilet paper.

Laa yujadu awraaq hammam.

لا يوجد أوراق الحمام.

I need some liquid soap, please.

Ahtaaju saabun saail, min fadlik.

أحتاج صابوناً سائلاً،من فضلك.

The water is very cold in the restrooms.

Al maa' baarid jidan fil hammaaamat.

الماء بارد جداً في الحمامات.

There is no hot water in these restrooms.

Laa yujadu maa' saakhin fii haadhihii al maraahidh.

لا يوجد ماء ساخن في هذه الحمامات.

The ladies' restrooms are always crowded!

Hammamu as-sayidaat daa'iman muzdahim.

حمام السيدات دائماً مزدحم.

The faucet is broken in the restroom.

Hanafiyatu al hammam maksuura.

حنفية الحمام مكسورة.

CULTURAL ETIQUETTE

Most people follow the Muslim practices of toilet etiquette; and it is common not to have toilet paper in the bathroom in households. You will have to learn to clean yourself with water using bidets—and your left hand, since you pick up food with your right—instead. Do not read, check your phone, answer calls or talk in the restroom. Make sure to wash your hands thoroughly with water and soap after using the toilet.

On the Telephone

KEY WORDS AND EXPRESSIONS

call (n.)	*ittisaal/mukaalamah*	اتصال/مكالمة
call (v.)	*yattasil*	يتّصل
local call	*mukaalamah mahalliyyah*	مكالمة محليّة
domestic phone call	*mukaalamah daakhiliyyah*	مكالمة داخليّة
international call	*mukaalamah duwaliyyah*	مكالمة دوليّة
phonecard	*bitaaqa hatifiy-yah*	بطاقة هاتفية
phone credit	*rasiid al hatif*	رصيد الهاتف
extension is busy	*al khat mashghuul*	الخط مشغول
Hello! (phone)	*aalo!*	آلو!
operator	*al muhawwil*	المحول
telephone	*tiliifuun/haatif*	تلفون/هاتف
telephone number	*raqam al haatif*	رقم الهاتف
mobile/cell phone	*haatif jaw-waal/naq-qaal*	هاتف جوال/نقال
Wi-Fi	*waay faay*	واي فاي
message	*risaalah*	رسالة
text	*nas*	نص
text message	*risaalah nas-siy-yah*	رسالة نصية
charger	*shaahin*	شاحن
iPhone	*ay fuun*	آي فون
server	*khaadim*	خادم

Hello, who is calling please? *Man 'alal-haatif?*
My name is Cheryl. *'Ismii Cheryl.*
Is Ayman there? *Hal Ayman mawjuud?*
No, he's away from his desk. *Laa, huwa layysa fii makatabihi.*
Please tell him I called. *Min fadlik akhbiriihi 'annanii ittasalt.*
My number is 324 7185. *Raqam haatifii huwu thalaathah, ithnataan, 'arba'ah, sab'ah, waahid thamaaniyah, khamsah.*
Certainly. I'll get him to call you back. *Akiid. Sa'ukhbiruhu anaki turidina an yatasil biki, inshaa'Alah.*

You have a phone call.

Ladayyka mukaalamah haatifiyyah.

لديك مكالمة هاتفية.

Just a moment, please.

Lahzah min fadlik. لحظة من فضلك.

Who is calling please? *Man yatakallam?* من يتكلم؟

Is Ayman there? *Hal Ayman mawjuud?* هل أيمن موجود؟

No, he is away from his desk.

Laa, laysaa fii maktabihi. لا، ليس في مكتبه.

He is out now. *Huwa bil khaarij al'aan.* هو بالخارج الآن.

He is on the other line.

Ma`ahuu mukaalamah 'ukhraa. معه مكالمة أخرى.

He is in a meeting now.

Huwa fii 'ijtimaa` al'aan. هو في اجتماع الآن.

Can I take a message? *Hal tawaddu 'an tatruka risaalah?*

هل تودّ أن تترك رسالة؟

Can I have him call you?

Aturiiduni an atluba minhu an yat-tasila bik?

أتريدني أن أطلب منه أن يتصل بك؟

Please tell him I called. *Qul lahu 'annii ittasalt min fadlik.*

قل له أني اتصلت من فضلك.

I want to make a phone call.

‘Uriidu ‘an ‘ujriya mukaalamah haatifiyyah.

أريد أن أجري مكالمة هاتفيّة.

I want to make an international phone call.

‘Uriidu ‘an ‘ujriya mukaalamah khaarijiyyah.

أريد أن أجري مكالمة دوليّة.

May I use your mobile phone, please?

Mumkin ‘an ‘astakhdima haatifakan naqqaal, law samaht? ممكن أن أستخدم هاتفك النّقّال، لو سمحت؟

My phone is out of battery.

Haatifii yahtaaj shahn. هاتفي يحتاج شحن.

Where can I get a data SIM card?

Min ayna ashtarii SIM card? من أين أشتري سيم كارد؟

Is there free Wi-Fi here?

Hal ‘yuujadu wayfay majaanii hunaa?

هل يوجد واي فاي مجاني هنا؟

Should I video call him/her?

Hal ‘at-tasil bihi/ biha bimukaalamat fiideo?

هل أتصل به/بها بمكالمة فيديو؟

What is your telephone number?

Maa raqmu haatifika? ما رقم هاتفك؟

My telephone number is… .

Raqmu haatifii huwa… . رقم هاتفي هو… .

I can't hear you well. ***Laa asma`u jayidan.*** لا أسمع جيداً.

There isn't a good connection.
Laa yujadu irsaalun jayid. لا يوجد إرسال جيد.

The connection is bad.
Al-irsaal ghayr jay-yid. الإرسال غير جيّد.

The line is disconnected. ***Inqata` al-khat.*** انقطع الخط.

The line is breaking up. ***Al-kalaam yataqata`.***
الكلام يتقطع.

PHRASES FOR SOCIAL MEDIA, APPLICATIONS, ETC.

Internet	*Shabakatul-Internet*	شبكة الانترنت
file/files	*malaff/malaf-faat*	ملف/ملفات
email	*al-bariid al-electrooni/iimiil*	البريد الإلكتروني/ إيميل
instant message	*risaalah fawriy-ya*	رسالة فورية
social media	*tawaasul ijtimaa`iy/ sushial miidiyaa*	تواصل اجتماعي/ سوشيل ميديا
social media network	*shabakatu at-tawaasul al ijtima`iy*	شبكة التواصل الاجتماعي
chat	*dardasha* (v)/*shaat*	دردشة/شات
chatting	*yudardish*	يدردش
Facebook	*Face buuk*	فيس بوك
Google+	*Guugal*	جوجل+
WhatsApp	*Watsup*	واتس آب
Line	*Khat*	خط

Twitter	*Twiiter*	تويتر
Snapchat	*Snaab tshaat*	سناب تشات
tweet	*taghrida*	تغريدة
tweet (v)	*ghr-rada/yughar-rid*	غرد/يغرد
hashtag	*haashtaaj*	هاش تاج
application/ applications	*tatbiiq/tatbiiqaat*	تطبيق/تطبيقات
app/apps	*aab/aabs*	آب/آبس
Facetime	*Fiistaaym*	فيس تايم
text message	*risaalah qasirah/ risaalah nas-siy-yah*	رسالة قصيرة/ رسالة نصيّة
selfie	*silfii*	سلفي
smartphone	*al-haatif adh-dhakii/ smaart fuun*	الهاتف الذكي/ سمارت فون
computer/ computers	*haasuub/hawaasib*	حاسوب/ حواسب
laptop	*al-haasuub al-mahmuul*	الحاسوب المحمول
charger	*shaahin bat-tariah*	شاحنة بطارية
videos	*ashritat al-fiidiyuu*	أشرطة فيديو
Youtube	*Yuutuub*	يوتوب
Apple	*Aable*	آبل
Windows	*Wiinduuz*	ويندوز
log/logging in	*tasjiil ad-dukhuul*	تسجيل الدخول
username	*ismul-mustakhdim*	اسم المستخدم
password	*kalimatus-sirr/ kalimatu al murur*	كلمة السّرّ/ كلمة المرور
blog	*bluugh/ mudawwinah*	بلوغ/مدونة
website	*mawqi` shabakatul-intarnit*	موقع شبكة الإنترنت

webpage	*safhat wib*	صفحة ويب
Instagram	*Instaghraam/ Instaqraam*	انستغرام/ انستقرام
spam	*sbam/muz`ij*	سبام/مزعج
hacking	*qarsanah*	قرصنة
block(ing)	*hajb/bluuk*	حجب/بلوك

Visiting an Office

KEY WORDS AND EXPRESSIONS

businessman	*rajul 'a`maal*	رجل أعمال
businesswoman	*sayyidat 'a`maal*	سيّدة أعمال
business hours	*saa`aat ad-dawaam ar-rasmiy*	ساعات الدوام الرسمي
company	*sharikah*	شركة
institution	*mu'assasah*	مؤسسة
office	*maktab*	مكتب
employee	*muwazzaf/`aamil*	موظف/عامل
employees	*muwazzafiin/`ummaal*	موظفين/عمال
job	*`amal/hirfah*	عمل/حرفة
career	*wazifah*	وظيفة
director	*mudiir*	مدير
conference room	*qaa`at mu'tamaraat/ ijtimaa`aat*	قاعة مؤتمرات/ اجتماعات
factory	*masna`*	مصنع
employer	*sahib al`amal*	صاحب العمل
profession	*mihnah/hirfah*	مهنة/حرفة
meeting	*ijtimmaa`*	اجتماع
invitation	*da`wah*	دعوة

capital (money)	*ra's maal*	رأس مال
consultant	*musta<u>sh</u>aar*	مستشار
distributor	*muazzi`*	موزع
vice president	*naa'ib ar-ra'iis*	نائب الرئيس
president	*ar-raiis*	الرئيس
representative	*muma<u>th</u>il*	ممثل
contract	*`aqd*	عقد
telephone	*haatif*	هاتف
fax	*faaks*	فاكس
e-mail address	*`unwaan bariid iliktruniy*	عنوان بريد إلكتروني
office	*maktab*	مكتب
director general	*mudiir `aam*	مدير عام
business manager	*mudiir al'a`maal*	مدير الأعمال
secretary	*assikretiirah*	السكرتيرة
director assistant	*naa'ib al mudiir*	نائب المدير
department head	*ra'iis al qism*	رئيس القسم
file	*malaff*	ملف
reception room	*qaa`atul-inti<u>z</u>aar*	قاعة الانتظار
interview	*muqaabalah*	مقابلة

I would like to meet... .
'Uriiduu 'an 'uqaabil... . أريد أن أقابل...

Where do you work? *'Ayna ta`mal?* أين تعمل؟

I work in... . *'Anaa 'a`malu fii... .* أنا أعمل في... .

What time does the conference start?
Mataa yabda' al mu'tamar? متى يبدأ المؤتمر؟

Please meet me at the hotel.
'Arjuu 'an tuqaabilanii fil funduq.
أرجو أن تقابلني في الفندق.

I have an important meeting.
`Indii ijtimaa`un muhim. عندي اجتماع مهم.

What time shall I come?
Mataa yajibu 'an 'aatii? متى يجب أن آتي؟

What time does the meeting start?
Mataa yabda'ul ijtimaa`? متى يبدأ الاجتماع؟

I am sorry to be late.
'Aasif 'ana muta'akh-khir. آسف، أنا متأخر.

What is the name of your company?
Masmu sharikatik? ما اسم شركتك؟

Where is your office? *'Ayna maktabuk?* أين مكتبك؟

What is your address? *Maa `unwaanuk?* ما عنوانك؟

What is your telephone number?
Maa raqmu haatifik? ما رقم هاتفك؟

Would you please write it down?
Saj-jilhu/'uktubhu lii law samaht?
سجله/اكتبه لي لوسمحت؟

I will give you a call. *Sa'attasil bik.* سأتصل بك.

Would you please call me?
Ittasil bii min fadlik? اتصل بي من فضلك؟

I would like to meet Mr. Abdullah.
'Awaddu 'an `uqaabil assayyid `Abdullah.
أودّ أن أقابل السيد عبد الله.

When can I meet Mr. Ahmed?
Mataa yumkinunii 'an 'uqaabilas sayyid 'Ahmad?
متى يمكنني أن أقابل السيد أحمد؟

Will 2 p.m. tomorrow be okay?
Hal assaa`ah ath-thaaniyah ghadan masaa'an waqtun munaasib? هل الساعة الثانية غداً مساءً وقت مناسب؟

Yes, that will be fine with me.
Na`am, haadhaa yunaasibunii. نعم، هذا يناسبني.

I have an appointment with Mr. Mohammad at 10 a.m.
`Indii maw`id ma`as sayyid Muhammad assaa`ah al`aashirah sabahan.
عندي موعد مع السيد محمد الساعة العاشرة صباحاً.

Where will the meeting be held?
'Ayna sayu`qadul ijtimaa`? أين سيعقد الاجتماع؟

Would you please tell him that I have arrived?
Mumkin 'an taquul lahu 'annii qad wasalt?
ممكن أن تقول له أني قد وصلت؟

My name is Paolo.
'Ismii Baawlu. اسمي باولو.

Yes, he is expecting me. We have an appointment.
Na`am, huwa yantazirunii, ladayynaa maw`id.
نعم، هو ينتظرني، لدينا موعد.

Can I use your telephone?
Mumkin 'an 'asta`mila haatifak?
ممكن أن أستعمل هاتفك؟

Can I wait here? *Hal mumkin 'an 'antazira hunaa?*
هل ممكن أن أنتظر هنا؟

At the Post Office

KEY WORDS AND EXPRESSIONS

mail	*bariid*	بريد
mail (v.)	*yursil bil barrid*	يرسل بالبريد
post office	*maktab bariid*	مكتب البريد
post officer	*muwazzaf al bariid*	موظف البريد
mail man	*saa`ii al bariid*	ساعي البريد
postcard	*bitaaqah baridiy-yah*	بطاقة بريدية

airmail	*bariid jawwii*	بريد جوي
express mail	*bariid musta`jal*	بريد مستعجل
registered mail	*bariid mussajjal*	بريد مسجل
letter	*risaalah*	رسالة
postal address	*‘unwaan baridiy*	عنوان بريدي
P.O. box	*sunduuq bariid*	صندوق بريد
stamp	*taabi`*	طابع
envelope	*zarf*	ظرف
send	*yursil*	يرسل
receive	*yastalim*	يستلم
parcel/package	*tard*	طرد
parcel	*turuud*	طرود
box	*`ulbah*	علبة
regular mail	*bariid `aadii*	بريد عادي
domestic	*mahal-lii*	محلي
international	*duwalii*	دولي
money order	*hawaala bariidiy-yah*	حوالة بريدية

Where is the nearest post office?
‘Ayna ‘aqrabu maktabi bariid? أين أقرب مكتب بريد؟

How do I get to the post office?
Kayfa ‘asilu ‘ilaa maktabil bariid?
كيف أصل إلى مكتب البريد؟

What time does the post office open?
Mataa yuftahu maktabul bariid? متى يفتح مكتب البريد؟

I need a stamp. *‘Ahtaaju ‘ilaa taabi`.* أحتاج إلى طابع.

I would like to send this to the U.S. by airmail.

'Awaddu 'an 'ursilahu 'ilaa 'Amriikaa bil bariid aljawwiyy. أودّ أن أرسله إلى أمريكا بالبريد الجوّيّ.

When does this shipment reach the U.K.?

Mataa ta<u>s</u>ilu haa<u>dh</u>ihi<u>sh</u>-<u>sh</u>u<u>h</u>nah 'ilaa Brii<u>t</u>aanyaa?
متى تصل هذه الشحنة إلى بريطانيا؟

I have a parcel to pick up.

`Indii <u>t</u>ard lit-tasliim. عندي طرد للتسليم.

I'd like to send international mail.

'Awaddu 'an 'ab`a<u>th</u>a bariid duwalii.
أودّ أن أبعث بريد دولي.

This is domestic mail.

Haa<u>dh</u>aa bariid ma<u>h</u>allii. هذا البريد محلي.

How much for a certified/registered mail?

Bikam al bariid al musajjal. بكم البريد المسجل.

When does the mail usually arrive?

Mataa ya<u>s</u>ilu al bariid `aadatan?
متى يصل البريد عادةً؟

Has the mailman come today?

Hal marra saa`iy al bariid al yawm?
هل مر ساعي البريد اليوم؟

Please take this mail to the post office.
Min fa<u>d</u>lik <u>kh</u>u<u>dh</u> al bariid 'ila maktab al bariid.
من فضلك خذ البريد إلى مكتب البريد.

This is regular mail. *Ha<u>dh</u>aa bariid `aadiy.* هذا بريد عادي.

Send this envelope by express mail.
Ib`a<u>th</u> haa<u>dh</u>aa a<u>z</u>arf bil bariid al musta`jal.
ابعث هذا الظرف بالبريد المستعجل.

Send this document by express mail.
Ib`a<u>th</u> haa<u>dh</u>ihil wa<u>th</u>iiqah bil bariid al musta`jal.
ابعث هذه الوثيقة بالبريد المستعجل.

I would like to send a money order.
'Uriidu an 'ursil <u>h</u>awaala baridiyyah.
أريد أن أرسل حوالة بريدية.

In the Bath

Public baths or ***hammams*** (or Turkish baths) are found in the Northern African regions and Arab countries like Algeria, Morrocco and Tunisia, located around the Mediterranean Sea. They are usually found in old cities and popular neighborhoods, as well as in hotels and spas. These can be found online or ask your hotel staff or tour guides for recommendations.

KEY WORDS AND EXPRESSIONS

bath/baths	*<u>h</u>ammaam/ <u>h</u>ammaamaat*	حمام/حمامات

private room	*ghurfah khaassah*	غرفة خاصة
hot water	*maa' saakhin*	ماء ساخن
cold water	*maa' baarid*	ماء بارد
soap	*saabuun*	صابون
towel	*minshafah*	منشفة
robe	*ruub*	روب
shampoo	*ghasuul/shambuu*	غسول/شامبو
clean	*naziif*	نظيف
wash (v.)	*ghasala*	غسل
hair	*sha`r*	شعر
massage	*dalk*	دلك
steam	*bukhaar (hammaam)*	بخار (حمام)
oils	*zuyuut*	زيوت
aroma/perfumes	*`utuur*	عطور
bathtub	*hawd al hammaam*	حوض الحمام
sink	*hawd*	حوض
mirror	*mir'aat*	مرآة

Where can I find a *hammam* in the area?

Ayana yujadu hammaam fii haadhihii al mantiqa?

أين يوجد حمام في هذه المنطقة؟

Is there a *hammam* in this hotel?

Hal yuujadu hammaam fii haadhaa al funduq?

هل يوجد حمام في هذا الفندق؟

Do you have *hammams* with private rooms?

Hal ladaikum hammaamaat bighuraf khaassah?

هل لديكم حمامات بغرف خاصة؟

Is the massage included in the rate?

Hal attadliik dimnas-si`r? هل التدليك ضمن السعر؟

What kind of oils do you use for the massage?

Ayu naw`in minaz-zuyuut tasta`miluuna lit-tadliik?

أي نوع من الزيوت تستعملون للتدليك؟

Do you use natural oils?

Hal tasta`maluun zuyuut tabii'iyyah?

هل تستعملون زيوت طبيعية؟

The water is very hot!

Al maa' saakhin jiddan! الماء ساخن جداً!

The water is too cold.

Al maa' baarid jiddan. الماء بارد جداً.

Do I need to stay in the steam room for a long time?

Hal ahtaaju 'an 'abqaaa fii ghuraft al bukhar limuddah tawiilah?

هل أحتاج أن أبقى في غرفة البخار لمدة طويلة؟

The room is very hot. Can I go to a colder room?

Al ghurfah saakhinah jid-dan. Mumukin an adhhab 'ila ghurfah baaridah?

الغرفة ساخنة جداً. ممكن أن أذهب إلى غرفة باردة؟

What kind of aroma/fragrance have you used?

'Ayyu naw` minal`utuur tastat`malun?

أي نوع من العطور تستعملون؟

Do you have hammams with private rooms? Hal ladaikum hammaamaat bighuraf khaassah?
Yes, we do. N'am. Yuujad.
HAMMAM RECEPTION
This is my first time in the hammam. Haadhihii awwal marrah lii fil-hammaam. What do I do next? Maadaa af'al?
Please go to the steam room. Min fadlik, idh-habii 'ilaa ghurfatil-bukhaar.
I will come to exfoliate your body and wash it. Sawfa aghsilu jismaki.
Then give you an oil massage. Wa ba'daha sa'udallikuki bizayt khaas.
How was it? Kayf kaan al hammaam?
The hammam was very relaxing! Al hammaam kaan murih jidan.
I will certainly come back again! Sa'arji`u marrah thaaniyah, bit-ta'kiid!

The steam is thick in this room!

Al bukhaar kathiif fi haadhihii al ghurfah!

البخار كثيف في هذه الغرفة!

This is my first time in the *hammam*.

Haadhihii awwal marrah lii fil-hammaam.

هذه أول مرة لي في الحمام.

What do I do next? *maadh af'alu alaan?*

ماذا أفعل الآن؟

The *hammam* was very relaxing.

Al hammaam kaana murih jidan. الحمام كان مريحاً جداً.

I will certainly come back again!

Sa'arji`u marrah thaaniyah, bit-ta'kiid!

سأرجع مرة ثانية بالتأكيد!

Housing

KEY WORDS AND EXPRESSIONS

to rent (v.)	*yasta'jir*	يستأجر
rent (n.)	*'iijaar*	إيجار
tenant	*musta'jir*	مستأجر
real estate agent	*wakiil `aqaariyy*	وكيل عقاريّ
landlord	*sahib al-bayyt*	صاحب البيت
deposit	*`arbuun*	عربون
lease contract	*`aqd isti'jaar*	عقد استئجار
signature	*tawqii`*	توقيع
unit	*wihdah sakaniyyah*	وحدة سكنية

residential area	*manṯiqah sakaniyyah*	منطقة سكنية
room/rooms	*g̲h̲urfah/g̲h̲uraf*	غرفة/غرف
kitchen	*maṯbak̲h̲*	مطبخ
bathroom/toilet	*h̲ammam*	حمّام
bedroom	*g̲h̲urfat nawm*	غرفة نوم
living room	*g̲h̲urfat juluus*	غرفة جلوس
guest room	*g̲h̲urfat d̲uyuuf*	غرفة ضيوف
hallway/corridor	*mamarr*	ممَرّ
house/houses	*bayt/buyout*	بيوت/بيت
apartment/ apartments	*s̲h̲aqqa/s̲h̲uqaq*	شقق/شقة
building/ buildings	*imaarah/imaaraat*	عمارات/عمارة

I want to rent an apartment.

'Uriidu 'an 'asta'jira s̲h̲aqqah. أريد أن أستاجر شقة.

*Usually male university students share apartments in big cities in Egypt.

Will there be any other tenants?

Hal yujad mu'ajiriin akhariin? هل يوجد مؤجرين آخرين؟

How much is the weekly rent?

Maa huwal 'iijaar al'usbuu`iyy?

ما هو الإيجار الأسبوعي؟

How much is the monthly rent?

Maa huwal 'iijaar as̲h̲-s̲h̲ahriyy?

ما هو الإيجار الشهري؟

How much is the yearly rent?

Maa huwal 'iijaar as-sanawiyy?

ما هو الإيجار السنويّ؟

I want a three-bedroom apartment.

'Uriidu shaqqah bi-thalaath ghuraf nawm.

أريد شقة بثلاث غرف نوم.

Does it have a separate bath?

Hal yuujadu hammaam munfasil?

هل يوجد حمام منفصل؟

Does the rent include the utility bills?

Hal yashmulu 'iijaar alfawatiir?

هل يشمل الإيجار الفواتير؟

What is the name of the complex?

Maa ismu haadhihi al wihdas-sakaniyyah?

ما اسم هذه الوحدة السكنية؟

Is there a balcony in the apartment?

Hal yujadu shurfa fish-shaqqah?

هل يوجد شرفة في الشقة؟

The house is beautiful but the kitchen is very small.

Shaq-qah jamiilah wa laakin al matbakh saghiir jidan.

البيت جميل ولكن المطبخ صغير جدا.

Is the dining room next to the kitchen?

Hall ghurfatu al-akl bi-jaanibil matbakh?

هل غرفة الأكل بجانب المطبخ؟

Does the kitchen open out to the dining room?

Haal al maṯbakh yaftah `alaa ghurfatil akl?

هل المطبخ يفتح على غرفة الأكل؟

Is there an elevator in this building?

Haal yujad mas`ad fii haadhihil `imaarah?

هل يوجد مصعد في هذه العمارة؟

What is the number of this building?

Maa huwaa raqamu haadihil `amaarah?

ما هو رقم هذه العمارة؟

What is the apartment number?

Maa huwa raqamush-shaq-qah? ما هو رقم الشقة؟

The house is very small!

Al baytu saghiir jidan! البيت صغير جداً!

Is there a storage room in this building?

Hal yujad makkan lit-takhziin fil `imaarah?

هل يوجد مكان للتخزين في العمارة؟

Visiting Someone's Home

There's a special place for receiving guests in most homes in Arab countries. This is usually either the whole ground floor on one side of the building, or a separate room close to the entrance in apartments, usually far from the living quarters to avoid interfering with the family's daily activities. The name of this room can vary from one country to another:

sitting area ***majlis*** مجلس (Gulf countries);
diwaniya ديوانية (Kuwait)
living room ****ghurfat aljuluus*** غرفة الجلوس (*Gulf countries)
guest room ***ghurfat ad-duyuuf*** غرفة الضيوف (Jordan, Syria, Palestine, Lebanon)
bedroom ***madaafah diiwaaniyyah*** مضافة ديوانية (Kuwait)

Although many Arab countries no longer prohibit mixing between men and women, mixing is still uncommon in other countries and conservative regions or families. If there's a function for the husband's guests, the female members of the family—wives and daughters—will often never make an appearance. Thus, male guests should not expect to be introduced to the ladies of the house. If the guests are a mixed group of foreigners, the females will gather in the living room, and the men in the guest room.

First-time guests are treated with extra special care and cordialty, and will be invited to sit next to the host. Refrain from bringing special dishes or bottles of alcohol; instead bring candy or homemade sweets. If you attend a party for a special occasion, i.e., someone's birthday, bring along a gift, but the recipient is unlikely to open it in front of you.

Remove your shoes before entering the house, guest room or reception room, unless the host says it's okay to wear shoes inside the house. When seated on the floor or on a chair, avoid pointing the soles of your feet towards your host—considered unclean and as an insult—and receive food or drink with your right hand.

KEY WORDS AND EXPRESSIONS

visit (n.)	***zi-yaarah***	زيارة
visit (v.)	***yazuur***	يزور
house	***bayt***	بيت
apartment	***shaq-qah***	شقة
guest/guests	***dayf/duyuuf***	ضيف/ضيوف
hospitality	***diyaafah***	ضيافة
generosity	***karam***	كرم
generous	***kariim***	كريم
Welcome!	***Ahlan!***	أهلاً!
directions	***ittijaahaat***	إتجاهات
way	***at-tariiq***	الطريق
beautiful/pretty	***jameel***	جميل
beautiful/pretty [fem.]	***jameelah***	جميلة
very	***jidan***	جداً

I will come visit (you) soon.
Sa'azuurukum `an qariib. سأزوركم عن قريب.

I will visit my friend tomorrow.
Sa'azuuru sadiiqii ghadan. سأزور صديقي غداً.

Yesterday I visted my friend (in his house).
Al'ams zurtu sadiiqii fi baytihi.
الأمس زرت صديقي في بيته.

Give me the directions to your house.
'A`tinii al ittijaahaat 'ilaa baytik.
أعطني الإتجاهات إلى بيتك.

Thanks for coming! Ahlan wasahlan. Come on in! Marhabaa… Al biit biitik…sharaftinaa, tafad-dalii!
You have a beautiful apartment! Shuqqatukum jamilah jidan!
Here's a small gift. Tafad-dalii, hadiya saghiirah.
You shouldn't have! Come, sit! Shukraan!Ma kaan 'alaiki. Ta'aaly, ijlisii.
Thanks for the meal! Shukran `alalat-ta`aam!
Please help yourself to more! Tafad-dalii, khudhii maziidan!
Thanks, I've had enough. Shukran laqad shabi`t.

You have a beautiful house!

Baytukum jamiilun jidan! بيتكم جميل جداً!

You have a beautiful apartment!

__Sh__aqqatukum jamilah jidan! شقتكم جميلة جداً!

Your house is close to work.

Baytukum qariibun minal`amal.

بيتكم قريب من العمل.

Is your house close to the university?

Hal baytukum qariib min al jaami`ah?

هل بيتكم قريب من الجامعة؟

Is your house close by?

Hal baytukum qariib? هل بيتكم قريب؟

Is your house far?

Hal baytukum ba`iid? هل بيتكم بعيد؟

How far is your house?

Kam yabu`du baytukum? كم يبعد بيتكم؟

Is your house in the city/downtown?

Hal baytukum fiil madiinah? هل بيتكم في المدينة؟

Hal baytukum fi wa__s__a__t__i al madiinah?

هل بيتكم في وسط المدينة؟

All praise to Allah, your house is big and beautiful!

Maa__sh__aa'a Allah, baytukum kabiir wa jamiil!

ما شاء الله، بيتكم كبير و جميل!

Medical Emergencies

KEY WORDS AND EXPRESSIONS

emergency room	*ghurfat tawaari'*	غرفة طوارئ
registration, reception	*al- istiqbaal*	الاستقبال
accident	*haadith*	حادث
nurse [FEMALE]	*mumarridah*	ممرضة
operation	*`amaliyyah*	عملية
patient	*mariid*	مريض
pharmacy	*sayydaliyyah*	صيدلية
pharmacist	*saydalaaniyy/saydaliy*	صيدلي/صيدلاني
medicine	*dawaa'*	دواء
doctor	*tabiib*	طبيب
dentist	*tabiib 'asnaan*	طبيب أسنان
pills	*hubuub*	حبوب
syrup	*sharaab*	شراب
eye drops	*qatrat `ayyn*	قطرة عين
mouth rinse	*ghasuul al fam*	غسول الفم
toothpaste	*ma`juun 'asnaan*	معجون أسنان
bandage	*dimaad*	ضماد
liquid	*saa'il*	سائل
treatment	*`ilaaj*	علاج
hospital	*mustashfaa*	المستشفى
pain	*waja`/alam*	وجع/ألم
body parts	*aa`daa' al jism*	أعضاء الجسم
head	*ra's*	رأس
eye	*`ayn*	عين
eyes	*`uyuun*	عيون

noise	*'anf*	أنف
mouth	*fam*	فم
ear	*'udhun*	أذن
ears	*'udhunaan*	أذنان
neck	*raqabah*	رقبة
shoulder	*katif*	كتف
shoulders	*katifaan*	كتفان
arm	*dhiraa`*	ذراع
arms	*dhiraa`ayn*	ذراعان
hand	*yad*	يد
hands	*yadaan*	يدان
wrist	*mi`sam*	معصم
wrists	*mi`samaan*	معصمان
finger	*'isba`*	إصبع
fingers	*asaabi`*	أصابع
back	*zahr*	ظهر
chest	*sadr*	صدر
stomach	*batn/ma`idah*	بطن/معدة
leg	*saaq*	ساق
legs	*saqaan*	ساقان
thigh	*fakhidh*	فخذ
thighs	*fakhidhaan*	فخذان
knee	*rukbah*	ركبة
knees	*rukbataan*	ركبتان
ankle	*kaahil*	كاحل
ankles	*kaahilaan*	كاحلان
foot	*qadam*	قدم
feet	*qadmaan*	قدمان
toe	*'isba` ar-rijl*	إصبع الرجل
toes	*asaabi` ar-rijl*	أصابع الرجل

[MALE] **I am sick.** ***'Anaa mariid.*** أنا مريض.

[FEMALE]] **I am sick.** ***'Anaa mariidah.*** أنا مريضة.

I do not feel well.
'Ana lastu `alaa maa yuraam. أنا لست على ما يرام.

It is very serious. ***'In-nahaa haalatun khatiirah* jiddan.***
إنها حالة خطيرة جداً.
* ***Khatiir*** means "dangerous" but "serious" in this context.

I have a… .	***`indii … .***	عندي… .
stomachache	***maghs***	مغص
headache	***sudaa`***	صداع
fever	***hummaa***	حمّى
heart condition	***marad fil qalb***	مرض في القلب
diabetes	***sukkarii***	سكري
blood pressure	***daght dam***	ضغط دم
chest pain	***'alam fis-sadr***	ألم في الصدر
diarrhea	***`is-haal***	إسهال

I feel dizzy. ***'Ash`uru bi dawkhah.*** أشعر بدوخة.

Where is the pharmacy?
'Aynas saydaliyyah? أين الصيدليّة؟

What time does the pharmacy open?
Mataa taftahus-saydaliyyah? متى تفتح الصيدلية؟

I would like something for a cold.
Uriiduu shay'an lil bard. أريد شيئاً للبرد.

I would like something for a cough.
`Uriidu shay'an lissu`aal. أريد شيئاً للسعال.

I have a toothache. *`Indii waja` 'asnaan.* عندي وجع أسنان.

I have broken a tooth.
Laqad kasartu sinnan. لقد كسرت سنّاً.

I have lost a filling.
Laqad faqadtul hashwah. لقد فقدت الحشوة.

I need to go to a dentist.
'Ahtaaju 'an 'adh-haba 'ilaa tabiibil 'asnaan.
أحتاج أن أذهب إلى طبيب الأسنان.

Is there a doctor who speaks English?
Hal yuujadu tabiibun yatakallamul injliiziyyah?
هل يوجد طبيب يتكلم الإنجليزية؟

Please call a doctor. *'Arjuu 'an tattasila bittabiib.*
أرجو أن تتصل بالطبيب.

Call a doctor quickly! *Ittasil bittabiib bisur`ah!*
اتصل بالطبيب بسرعة!

Have you called a doctor yet?
Halit tasalta bittabiib ba`d? هل اتصلت بالطبيب بعد؟

Call a dentist, please. *Ittasil bi tabiibil 'asnaan min fadlik.*
اتصل بطبيب الأسنان من فضلك.

I want to go to a dentist.

'Uriidu 'an 'adh-haba 'ilaa tabiibi 'asnaan.

أريد أن أذهب إلى طبيب أسنان.

Is there a dentist near here?

Hal yuujadu tabiibu 'asnaan qariib min hunaa?

هل يوجد طبيب أسنان قريب من هنا؟

Can you recommend a dentist?

Hal tuusii bi tabiibi 'asnaan? هل توصي بطبيب أسنان؟

I need to go to the hospital.

'Ahtaaju 'an 'adh-haba 'ilal mustashfaa.

أحتاج أن أذهب إلى المستشفى.

We took him/her to the hospital.

'akhadhnaa(hu)/(haa) 'ilal mustashfaa.

أخذناه/ها إلى المستشفى.

Let's go to another hospital.

Fal nadh-hab 'ilaa mustashfan 'aakhar.

فلنذهب إلى مستشفى آخر!

Is there a children's hospital here?

Hal yuujadu mustashfaa 'atfaal hunaa?

هل يوجد مستشفى أطفال هنا؟

I am at the hospital.

'Anaa bil mustashfaa. أنا بالمستشفى.

Is there a nearby hospital?

Hal yuujadu mustashfaa qariib?

هل يوجد مستشفى قريب؟

Take me to the hospital.

Khudhnii 'ilal mustashfaa. خذني إلى المستشفى.

Please call an ambulance.

Rajaa'an ittasil bisayyaratil 'is`aaf.

رجاءً اتصل بسيارة الإسعاف.

It's urgent, we need an ambulance.

'Innahaa haalah taari'ah, nahtaaju 'ilaa sayyarati 'is`aaf. إنها حالة طارئة، نحتاج إلى سيارة إسعاف.

Take her/him to the hospital.

Khudh(haa)/(hu) `ilal-mustashfaa (fem./masc.).

خذ(ها)/(ه) إلى المستشفى.

She/He was hit by a car, please call an ambulance.

Sadamathaa sayyaarah, ittasil bi sayyaratil 'is`aaf min fadlik. صدمتها سيارة، اتصل بسيارة الإسعاف من فضلك.

What is the ambulance number?

Maa raqmu sayyaratil 'is`aaf? ما رقم سيارة الإسعاف؟

Have you called an ambulance yet?

Halit tasalta bisayyaratil 'is`aaf ba`d?

هل اتصلت بسيارة الإسعاف بعد؟

PART THREE
Key Names & Places

USEFUL KEY WORDS

place	*makaan*	مكان
places	*amaakin*	أماكن
country	*balad*	بلد
countries	*buldaan*	بلدان
area	*mintaqah*	منطقة
areas	*manaatiq*	مناطق
region	*nahiyah*	ناحية
regions	*nahiya/nawaahi*	نواحي
state	*wilaayah*	ولاية
states	*wilayaat*	ولايات
sheikhdom*	*imaarah*	إمارة
	imaarat sheikhdoms	إمارات

*ruled by a Sheikh or Amiir/Prince

kingdom	*mamlakah*	مملكة
republic	*jumhuriyah*	جمهورية
capital (city)	*`aasimah*	عاصمة
city	*maddiinah*	مدينة
village	*qariyah*	قرية
neighborhood	*hay/haarah*	حي/حارة

downtown	*wasat al madinah /al balad*	وسط المدينة/ البلد
desert	*sahra'*	صحراء
mountain	*jabal*	جبل
sea coast	*as-sahil*	الساحل
valley	*waadii*	وادي
island	*jaziirah*	جزيرة
islands	*juzur*	جزر
peninsula	*shibh jaziirah*	شبه جزيرة
gulf	*khaliij*	خليج

COUNTRIES, ISLANDS & REGIONS

ALGERIA	*al-jazaa'ir*	الجزائر
Algiers [CAPITAL]	*al-jazaa`ir*	الجزائر
Oran	*wahraan*	وهران
Tlemcen	*tilimsaan*	تلمسان
Constantine	*qasantiinah*	قسنطينة
Annaba	*`annaabah*	عنابة
Skikda	*skiikdah*	سكيكدة
Al Ouana [ISLAND]	*al`awanah*	العوانة
Rachgoun [ISLAND]	*rashquun*	رشقون
BAHRAIN	*al-bahrayn*	البحرين
Manamah [CAPITAL]	*al-manaamah*	المنامة
Almuharraq	*al-muharraq*	المحرق
Sitra [ISLAND]	*jaziiratu sitrah*	جزيرة سترة
Muharraq Island	*jaziiratu ai-muharraq*	جزيرة المحرق
COMOROS	*juzur al-qumur*	جزر القمر
Moroni [CAPITAL]	*murunii*	موروني
Anjouan [ISLANDS]	*anjuwaan*	أنجوان

DJIBOUTI	*jiibuutii*	جيبوتي
Djibouti [CAPITAL]	*jiibuutii*	جيبوتي
EGYPT	*misr*	مصر
Cairo [CAPITAL]	*al-qaahirah*	القاهرة
Alexandra	*al-iskandariyyah*	الإسكندرية
Ismaeliyya	*al-isma`iiliyyah*	الإسماعيلية
Aswan	*aswaan*	أسوان
El-Suwies	*as-suwais*	السويس
Dumyat	*dimyaat*	دمياط
Sanafir Island	*jaziiratu sanaafiir*	جزيرة صنافير
Tiran Island	*jaziratut-tiiraan*	جزيرة التيران
IRAQ	*al-`iraaq*	العراق
Baghdad [CAPITAL]	*baghdaad*	بغداد
Mousel	*al-muusil*	الموصل
Basrah	*al-basrah*	البصرة
Nassiriyyah	*an-naasiriyyah*	الناصرية
Najaf	*an-najaf*	النجف
Kirkuk	*karkuuk*	كركوك
Dihok/Duhok	*dihuuk*	دهوك
Arbil/Erbil	*arbiil*	أربيل
JORDAN	*al-urdun*	الأردن
Amman [CAPITAL}	*`ammaan*	عمان
Irbid	*irbid*	إربد
Zerka	*az-zarqaa'*	الزرقاء
Jerash	*jarash*	جرش
Karak	*al-karak*	الكرك
KUWAIT	*al-kuwayt*	الكويت
Kuwait [CAPITAL]	*al-Kuwayt*	الكويت

Bubiyan [ISLANDS]	*jaziiratu buubiyaan*	جزيرة بوبيان
Failaka [ISLANDS]	*jaziiratu filkaa*	جزيرة فيلكا
Umm Al Maradim	*ummul maraadim*	أم المرادم
LEBANON	*lubnaan*	لبنان
Beirut [CAPITAL]	*bayruut*	بيروت
Tripoli	*taraablus*	طرابلس
Sidon	*saydaa*	صيدا
Tyre	*suur*	صور
Baalbeck	*b`albak*	بعلبك
LIBYA	*liibyaa*	ليبيا
Tripoli [CAPITAL]	*taraablus*	طرابلس
Banghazi [CAPITAL]	*banghaazii*	بنغازي
Tubruq	*tubruq*	طبرق
Farwah [ISLANDS]	*jaziiratu farwah*	جزيرة فروة
MAURITANIA	*muriitaanyaa*	موريتانيا
Nouakchott [CAPITAL]	*nawaakshut*	نواكشوط
Chanqit	*shanqiit*	شنقيط
Arguin [ISLANDS]	*jaziirat araghiin*	جزيرة أرغين
MOROCCO	*al-maghrib*	المغرب
Rabat	*ar-rabat*	الرباط
Casablanca	*ad-daar al-baydaa'*	الدار البيضاء.
Marrakech	*maraakish*	مراكش
Fes	*faas*	فاس
Meknas	*maknaas*	مكناس
Aghadir	*'aghaadiir*	أغادير

OMAN	*`umaan*	عمان
Muscat	*masqat*	مسقط
Salalah	*salaalah*	صلالة
Sour	*suur*	صور
Telegraph [ISLANDS]	*jaziiratu*	جزيرة
	at-tilighraaf	التلغراف
Palestine	*falastiin*	فلسطين
Jerusalem	*al-quds*	القدس
Ramallah	*raamallah*	رام الله
Bethlehem	*bait-lahim*	بيت لحم
Nablus	*naablis*	نابلس
Gaza	*ghazzah*	غزة
Hebron	*al-khaliil*	الخليل
Jenin	*jiniin*	جنين
Toulkarem	*tuulkarim*	طولكرم
Jericho	*'ariihaa*	أريحا
QATAR	*qatar*	قطر
Doha [CAPITAL]	*ad-dawhah*	الدوحة
Halul Island	*jaziirat haaluul*	جزيرة حالول
SAUDI ARABIA	*as-su`uudiyyah*	السعودية
Riyadh [CAPITAL]	*ar-riyaad*	الرياض
Mecca	*makkah*	مكة
Medina	*al-madiinah*	المدينة المنورة
	al-munaw-warah	
Jeddah	*jaddah*	جدة
Dammam	*d-dammaam*	الدمام
Abha	*abhaa*	أبها

Tabouk	*tabuuk*	تبوك
Tarout [ISLAND]	*jaziirat taaruut*	جزيرة تاروت
SOMALIA	*as-suumaal*	الصومال
Mogadishu [CAPITAL]	*maqadiishu*	مقديشو
Berbera	*barbarah*	بربرة
SUDAN	*as-suudaan*	السودان
Khartoum [CAPITAL]	*al-khurtuum*	الخرطوم
Omdurman	*umm durmaan*	أم درمان
Juba	*juubaa*	جوبا
SYRIA	*suuryaa*	سوريا
Damascus [CAPITAL]	*dimashq*	دمشق
Aleppo	*halab*	حلب
Latakia	*al-laadhiqiyyah*	اللاذقية
Homs	*hims*	حمص
Palmyra	*tadmur*	تدمر
Al-Hasakeh	*al-hasakih*	الحسكة
Tartous	*tartuus*	طرطوس
Banyas	*baanyaas*	بانياس
Arwad Island	*jaziratu arwaad*	جزيرة أرواد.
TUNISIA	*tuunis*	تونس
Tunis [CAPITAL]	*Tuunis*	تونس
Bizerte	*binzart*	بنزرت
Sfax	*safaaqis*	صفاقس
Sousse	*suusa*	سوسة
Gabes	*qaabis*	قابس
Monastir	*al-munastiir*	المنستي

Kairouan	*al-qayrawaan*	القيروان
Jerba	*jirbah*	جربة
Tabarka	*tabarqa*	طبرقة
UNITED ARAB EMIRATES	*al-imaaraat al-mutahidah*	الإمارات المتحدة
Abu Dhabi [CAPITAL]	*abuu-zabii*	أبو ظبي
Dubai	*dubayy*	دبي
Sharja	*ash-shaariqah*	الشارقة
El-Ein	*al-`iyn*	العين
Ajman	*`ajmaan*	عجمان
El-Fujeirah	*al-fujairah*	الفجيرة
Ras El-Kheimah	*ra's al-khaimah*	رأس الخيمة
Abu Musa [ISLAND]	*jaziirat abu mussaa*	جزيرة أبو موسى
Alddaiya	*addab`iyyah*	الضبعية
YEMEN	*al-yaman*	اليمن
Sana'a [CAPITAL]	*san`aa'*	صنعاء
Aden	*`adan*	عدن
Ta'az	*ta'z*	تعز
Hanish [ISLANDS]	*juzur haniish*	جزر حنيش

NAMES IN DUBAI

Dubai is the largest emirate and one of the seven emirates that make up the country.

Dubai	*Dubayy*	دبي
Ras Al Khor	*raas alkhoor*	راس الخور
Djabel Ali	*jabel 'ali*	جبل علي

Bur Dubai	*buur dubay*	بور دبي
Deira	*deyra*	ديرة
Wafi City	*madinat waafii/ waafii citii*	مدينةوافي/وافي ستي
Jumeirah	*jumeirah*	جميرا
Satwa	*as-satwa*	السطوة

PLACES IN ABU DHABI

Abu Dhabi is one of the seven emirates that make up The United Arab Emirates. It is also the capital of the EAU and the Emirate of Abu Dhabi itself.

Abu Al	*abu al-abyad*	أبو الأبيض
Al Arayam Island	*jazeeratul aryaam*	جزيرة الأريام
Dalma	*jaziiratu dalmaa*	جزيرة دلما
Al Mushrif	*al-mushrif*	المشرف
Al Gharbiya	*al-gharbiya*	الغربية
Madinat Zayed	*aadinat zaayad*	مدينة زايد
Al Ruyais	*arruyais*	الرويس
Ghayathi	*ghayaathi*	غياثي
Liwas (Oasis)	*waahat liwaa*	واحة ليوا
Sila	*as-sila`*	السلع
Khalifa City	*madinat khaliifah*	مدينة خليفة

DEPARTMENT STORES AND SHOPPING CENTERS

World Trade Center Mall	*suuq markaz ettijaarah al ` aalamiy*	سوق مركز التجارة العالمي
Abu Dhabi Mall	*abu zabi muul*	أبو ظبي مول

Marina Mall	*marina muul*	مارينا مول
Al Wahda Mall	*al wahda muul*	الوحدة مول

Madinat Zayed Shopping and Gold Center
markez madinat zaayed attijaarii wa marks adhahab walmujawharaat
مركز مدينة زايد التجاري و مركز الذهب و المجوهرات

Hamdan Mall	*hamdaan muul*	حمدان مول
Foutouh Al Khayr Mall	*fuutuuh al khayr muul*	فتوح الخير مول
Mazyad Mall	*mazyad muul*	مزيد مول
Dalma Mall	*dalam muul*	دلمةمول
Al Ain Mall	*al`ayn muul*	العين مول

INDUSTRIAL ZONES

Khalifa Industrial Zone (Kizad)	*madinat khalifa as-sina`iyah*	مدينة خليفة الصناعية
Ras Al Khor	*raas al-khuur as-sina`iyah*	رأس الخور الصناعية
Al Quoz /Al Goze Industrial Area (Dubai)	*mantiqa al-quuz*	منطقة القوز
Al Kubaisi	*al-qubaisii*	القبيسي
Al Safaa Area	*mantiqat as-safah*	منطقة الصفة

OTHER USEFUL TRAVEL INFORMATION

trip	safar	سفر
trips	asfaar	أسفار
business mission	muhim-mah tijariy-yah	مهمة تجارية
travel for studies	safar li-d-diraasah	سفر للدراسة
medical trip	safar ṭib-biy	سفر طبي
medical mission	muhimmah ṭib-biy-yah	مهمة طبية
tourist	saai'ḥ	سائح
tourist [fem.]	saai'ḥah	سائحة
tourists	suy-yaaḥ	سياح
passport	jawaaz safar	جواز سفر
embassy	sifaarah	سفارة
consulate	qunṣuliyah	قنصلية
visa	ta'shiirah	تأشيرة
residence	iqaamah	إقامة

MAJOR NEWSPAPERS

Gulf News	juulf nyuuz	جولف نيوز
Akhbar Al Arab	akhbaar al`arab	أخبارالعرب
Al Itihad	Al Itiḥaad	الإتحاد
Awraaq	awraaq	أوراق
The National	dha nashionaal	ذا ناشيونال
Khaleej Times	khaliij timez	خليج تايمز

POPULAR WEBSITES

http://government.ae/en/ http://visitabudhabi.ae/en/default.aspx
http://www.dubai.ae/en/Pages/default.aspx

English-Arabic Dictionary

A

about حوالي/تقريباً *taqriiban/ hawaalay*
above على/فوق *fawqa/`ala*
abroad خارج البلاد *khaarij al-bilaad*
accident حادث *hadith*
adaptor واصلة *wasla*
address عنوان *`unwaan*
admission دخول/قبول *dukhuul/ qabuul*
admission price سعر الدخول *s`ir ad-ukhuul*
adult بالغ\كهل *baaligh/kahl*
advice نصيحة *nasiiha*
after بعد *ba`d*
afternoon مساء *massa'*
aftershave كولونيا *kulunya*
again مرة أخرى *marra ukhraa*
against مقابل\ضد *muqaabil/did*
age عمر *`umr*
AIDS إيدز *aydz*
air هواء *hawaa'*
air conditioning تبريد *tabriid*
airmail بريد جوي *bariid jawwii*
airplane طائرة *taa'ira*
airport مطار *mataar*
alarm إنذار *indhaar*
alarm clock ساعة تنبيه/منبه *saa`at tanbiih/munabbih*
alcohol الكحول *al-kuhuul*
all الكل *alkul*
all day كل اليوم *kul al-yawm*
all the time طول الوقت *tuul al-waqt*
allergy حساسية *hasaasiy-yah*
alone وحيد/وحيدة *wahiid/ wahiida* (f.)
altogether جميعاً/مع بعض *jamii`an/ma` ba`d*
always دائماً *daa'iman*
ambassador سفير *safiir*
ambulance سيارة إسعاف *sayyaarat is`aaf*
America أمريكا *amriika*
American أمريكي *amariikiy*
American (f.) أمريكية *amariikiy-yah*
amount كمية *kammiyya*
amusement park حديقة ملاهي *hadiiqatu malaahii*
anesthetic (general) تخدير *takhdiir*
anesthetic (local) تخدير موضعي *takhdiir mawdi`ii*
angry غاضب/منفعل *ghaadib/ munfa`il*
animal حيوان *hayawaan*
ankle كعب *ka`ib*
answer جواب *jawaab (rad)*
ant نملة *namla*
antibiotics مضاد حيوي *mudaad hayawii*
antifreeze مضاد للتجميد *mudaad lit-tajmiid*

antique قديم *qadiim*
antiques تحف *tuhaf*
antiseptic مضاد للعفونة *mudaad lil`ufuunah*
anus الشرج *ash-sharj*
apartment شقة للسكن *shaqqa lissakan*
aperitif مشهي *mushahhi*
apologies اعتذار *i`tidhaar*
apple تفاحة *tuffaaha*
apple juice عصير تفاح *`asiir tuffaah*
appointment موعد *maw`id*
April نيسان/أبريل *abriil /naysaan*
architecture هندسة معمارية *handasa mi`maariya*
area مساحة/منطقة *masaaha/ mintaqa*
area code (mail) مفتاح بريدي *miftaah bariidii*
area code (phone) مفتاح المنطقة *miftaah al-mintaqa*
arm ذراع *dhiraa`*
arrange يرتب *yurattib*
arrive يصل *yasil*
arrow سهم *sahm*
art فن *fan*
art gallery معرض للفنون *ma`rad lilfunun*
artery شريان *shuryaan*
article مقال *maqaal*
artificial اصطناعي *istinaa`iy*
artificial respiration التنفس الاصطناعي *at-tanaffus al-istinaa`ii*
ash رماد *ramaad*
ashtray منفضة سجائر *minfadat sajaa'ir*
ask سأل/يسأل *yas'al/sa'la*
ask for يطلب *yatlub*
aspirin أسبرين *asbiriin*
assault اعتداء *i`tidaa'*
assorted مصنف *musannaf*
at home في البيت *fii al-bayt*
at night في الليل *fii al-layl*
at the back في الخلف *fii al-khalf*
at the front في الأمام *fii al-amaam*
at the latest في الآخر *fii al aakhir*
at the least على الأقل *`alaa al-qal*
aubergine باذنجان *badhinjaan*
August آب/أغسطس *aghustus/ aab*
Australia أستراليا *ustiraaliyaa*
Australian أسترالي *ustiraaliy*
Australian أسترالية *ustiraaliy-yah*
auto سيارة *say-yaarah*
automatic آلي/أوتوماتيكي *aali/ utumaatiikii*
automobile سيارة *say-yaarah*
autumn الخريف *al-khariif*
awake مستيقظ *mustayqiz*
aware مدرك *mudrik*
awareness إدراك/وعي *idraak/wa`y*
awe اندهاش *indihaash*
awesome مدهش/رائع *mudhish/ raai`*
awful فظيع *fazii`*
awning مظلة *mizalah*

B

baby رضيع/طفل *radii`/tifl*
baby food طعام طفل *ta`aam tifl*
babysitter حاضنة *haadina*
back (part of body) ظهر *zahr*
back (rear) خلف *khalf*
backpack حقيبة ظهر *haqibatu zahr*
backpacker سائح مترجل *saa'ih mutarrajil*
bad (rotting/terrible) فاسد/سيئ *faasid; sayyi'*
bag حقيبة *haqiiba*
baggage أمتعة *amti`a*
baker خباز *khabbaaz*
balcony شرفة *shurfa*
ball كرة *kura*
ballpoint pen قلم جاف *qalam jaaf*
banana موز *mawz*
bandage ضامد *dimaad*
bandaids ضمادات *damaadaat*
bang ضربة شديدة *darba shadiida*
bangs انفجارات *infijaraat*
bank (finance) مصرف/بنك *bank/masraf*
bank (river) ضفة *diffah*
barbecue شواء في الهواء الطلق *shiwaa' fii al-hawaa' at-talq*
basketball كرة السلة *kurat as-salla*
bath حمام *ham-maam*
bathmat فرشة باب الحمام *farshat baab al-ham-maam*
bathrobe رداء حمام *ridaa' ham-maam*
bathroom غرفة الحمام *ghurfat al-ham-maam*
bath towel منشفة حمام *minshafat ham-maam*
battery بطارية *bat-taariyah*
beach شاطئ *shaati'*
beans فاصوليا *faasuuliyah*
beautiful جميل *jamiil*
beautify تجميل *tajmiil*
beauty جمال *Jamaal*
bed سرير *sariir*
bedding مفرشة السرير *mafruushaat as-sariir*
bedroom غرفة النوم *ghrfatun-nawm*
bee نحلة *nahla*
beef لحم بقر *lahm baqar*
beehive خلية النحل *khaliyatu an-nahl*
begin بدأ *bada'*
beginning بداية *bidaayah*
behind خلف *khalf*
belt حزام *hizaam*
berth رصيف ميناء/مرسى *rasiif miinaa'/marsaa*
better (to get) حسن *has-san*
bicycle دراجة *dar-raaja*
bikini البكيني *al-bikiinii*
bill فاتورة *fatuura*
billiards بليارد *bilyaard*
birth ميلاد *miilaad*
birthday يوم الميلاد *yawm al-miilaad*
biscuit بسكويت *baskawiit*
bite لدغة *ladgha*
bitter مر *mur*

black أسود *aswad*
black and white أسود و أبيض *aswad wa abyad*
bland (taste) بلا طعم *bilaa ta`am*
blanket بطانية *battaaniyya*
bleach مبيض *mubayyid*
bleed ينزف *yanzif*
blind (can't see) أعمى *a`maa*
blind (window) ستارة *sitaara*
blisters بثور جلدية *buthuur jildiyyah*
blond أشقر *ashkar/shqraa'* (f.)
blood دم *dam*
blood pressure ضغط الدم *daght ad-dam*
bloody nose نزيف دم *naziif anf*
blouse بلوزة *blouzah*
blue أزرق *azraq*
boat قارب *qaarib*
body جسم *jism*
boiled مغلي *maghlii*
bone عظم *`azm*
book كتاب *kitaab*
booked, reserved محجوز *mahjuuz*
booking office مكتب حجز *maktab hajz*
bookshop مكتبة *maktabah*
border حد *had*
bored سائم *sa'im (dajir)*
boring ممل *mumil*
born مولود *mawluud*
borrow يستأجر *yasta'iir*
botanic gardens حدائق نباتية *hadaa'iq nabaatiyya*
both كلاهما *kilaahuma*
bottle (baby's) زجاجه طفل/قنينة *qin-niinah/zuzajat tifl*
bottle-warmer مسخن قنينة *musakhin qinniina*
box صندوق *sunduuq*
box office صندوق البريد *sunduuq bariid*
boy ولد *walad*
boyfriend صديق *sadiiq*
bra(s) صدرية/صدريات *sadriyya/sadriyaat*
bracelet سوار *siwaar*
braised مطبوخ ببطء *matbakh bibut'*
brake مكابح/فرامل *faraamil/makaabih*
brake oil زيت فرامل *zayt faraamil*
bread خبز *khubz*
break استراحة *istiraaha*
breakfast فطور/إفطار *fatuur/iftaar*
breast ثدي/صدر *thadiy/sadr*
breast (chicken) صدر *sadr*
breast milk حليب الصدر/حليب الأم *haliib thadii/haliib al'um*
bridge جسر *jisr*
briefs ملخص *mulakhas*
bring يجلب *yajlib*
brochure منشور *manshuur*
broken مكسور/عاطل *maksuur/`aatil*
bronze نحاس/برونز *brunz/nuhaas*
broth حساء *hisaa'*
brother أخ *akh*
brown بني *bunnii*

bruise كدمة *kadma*
brush فرشاة *furshaat*
bucket سطل/دلو *dalw/satl*
buffet خزانة *khizaanah*
bugs بق *baq*
building بناية *binaaya*
bun تسريحة *tasriiha*
burglary سطو *satw (sariqa)*
burn (injury) حرق *harq*
burn (v.) يحرق/يحترق *yuhriq/yahtariq*
burnt محروق *mahruuq*
bus حافلة (باص) *haafila (baas)*
bus station محطة حافلات *mahattat haafilaat*
bus stop موقف حافلة *mawqif haafila*
business card بزنس كارد *bizness kaart*
business class درجة أعمال *darajat a`maal*
business trip رحلة عمل *rihlat `amal*
busy (schedule) مشغول *mashghuul*
busy (traffic) ازدحام *izdihaam*
butcher قصاب (جزار) *qassaab (jazaar)*
butter زبدة *zubda*
button زر *zirr*
by airmail بالبريد الجوي *bil-bariid al-jawwii*
by phone بالتلفون/بالهاتف *bit-tilifuun/bilhatif*

C

cab طاكسي/سيارة أجرة *taxi/siyaarat ujrah*
cabbage ملفوف *malfuuf*
cabin كوخ *kuukh*
cake كعك *ka`k*
call (phone call) مكالمة *mukaalamah*
call (to phone) يتصل *yattasil*
camera آلة التصوير/كامرا *kaamira/aalatut taswiir*
camping مخيم *mukhayyam*
can يستطيع *yastatii`*
can opener مفتاح علب *miftaah `ulab*
canal (waterway) قناة *qanaah*
cancel يلغي *yulghii*
candle شمعة *sham`a*
candy حلوة *halwaa*
car سيارة *sayyaara*
car charger شاحنة السيارة *shaahin as-saiyara*
car documents أوراق السيارة *awraaqu as-say-yaara*
car seat (child's) مقعد طفل *maq`ad tifl*
car trouble عطب في السيارة *`atab fii as-sayyaara*
cardigan سترة صوف *sutrat suuf*
careful حاذر *hadhir*
carpet سجادة *sajjaada*
carriage عربة *`araba*
carrot جزر *jazar*
cartridge خرطوشة *khartuusha*
cash فلوس/سيولة/كاش/نقدي *fuluus/suyuulah/kaash/naqdii*

cash card بطاقة نقد *bitaaqat naqd*
cash desk مكتب تصريف *maktab tasriif*
cash machine آلة تصريف *aalat tasriif*
casino كازينو *kaaziinu*
castle قصر *qasr*
cat قط *qit*
cat (f.) قطة *qit-tah*
catalog كتالوغ *kataluug*
cauliflower قرنبيط *qarnabiit*
cause سبب *sabab*
cave كهف *kahf*
CD قرص *qurs*
celebrate يحتفل *yahtafil*
cell phone محمول/جوال *mahmoul/jawwal*
cemetery مقبرة *maqbara*
center (middle) مركز *markaz*
center (of city) مركز/وسط المدينة *markaz/wasat al-madiina*
centimeter سنتمتر *sintimitar*
central مركزي *markaziy*
central heating تدفئة مركزية *tadfi'a markaziyya*
certificate وثيقة/شاهدة *wathiiqa/shahaada*
chair كرسي *kursii*
chambermaid خادمة فندق *khaadimatu funduq*
change (money) صرف *sarf*
change (trains) تغيير *taghyiir*
change the baby's diaper يغير حفاظ الطفل *yughayyir haffad at-tifl*
change the oil يغير الزيت *yughayyir az-zayt*
charger شاحن *shaahin*
charter flight رحلة جوية مؤجرة *rihla jaw-wiy-yah mu'aj-jarah*
chat دردشة *dardasha*
check (bill) مراجعة الفاتورة *muraaja`at alfaatuurah*
check (n.) فحص *fahs*
checked luggage فحص الحقائب/الأمتعة *alamti`ah/fahs al-haqaa'ib*
check in النزول بالفندق *an-nuzuul bil-funduq*
check out مغادرة الفندق *mughadarat al-funduq*
Cheers! صحتين *Sahtiin!*
cheese جبن/جبنة *jubn/jubnah*
chef شيف/كبير الطباخين *shiif/kabiir at-tabbaakhiin/tabaakh*
chess شطرنج *shitranj*
chewing gum علك/لبان *lubaan/`ilk*
chicken دجاج *dajaaja*
chickpea(s) حمص *hummus*
child طفل *tifl*
child's seat (in car) مقعد طفل *maq`ad tifl*
chilled مجمد *mujam-mad*
chimney مدخنة *midkhanah*
chin ذقن *dhaqn*
China (country) الصين *Es-siin*
chocolate شوكولاطة *shuukalaata*
choice اختيار *ikhtiyaar*
choose اختار *ikhtaar*
choose (v.) اختار/يختار *ikhtaara/yakhtar*

chop يقطع/قطع *'qata`a /yaqta`*
chopsticks أعواد صينية *a`waad siiniyyah*
church كنيسة *kaniisah*
church service صلاة الكنيسة *salaat al-kaniisa*
cigar سيجار *siijaar*
cigarette سيجارة *siijaara*
circle دائرة *daa'ira*
circus سيرك *siirk*
citizen مواطن *muwaatin*
citizenship جنسية *jinsiy-yah*
city مدينة *madiina*
clean نظيف *naziif*
clean (v.) نظف/ينظف *yunaz-zif/naz-zaf*
cleaner منظف *munaz-zif*
clear واضح *waadih*
clear (color) شفاف *shaffaaf*
clearance (sale) تصفية *tasfiya*
clock ساعة (جدران) *saa`at (juduraan)*
close قريب *qariib*
closed مغلق *mughlaq*
closed off (road) مغلق *mughlaq*
clot جلطة/تجلط *jalta/tajallut*
cloth قماش *qumash*
clothes ملابس *malaabis*
clothes dryer مجفف الغسيل *mujaffif al ghasiil*
clothes hanger شماعة *sham-maa`ah*
clothing ملابس/ثياب *malaabis/thiyaab*
clutch (car) دواسات القابض *dawaasat l-qaabid*
coat جاكيت/سترة *jakiet/sitra*
coat (overcoat) معطف *mi`taf*
coating طلاء *tilaa'*
cockroach صرصور *sarsuur*
cocoa كاكاو *kakaw*
coffee قهوة *qahwa*
cold (not hot) بارد *baarid*
cold, flu انفلونزا *influwanza*
collar ياقة *yaaqa*
collarbone الترقوة *at-turquwa*
colleague/colleague (f.) زميل/زميلة *zamiil/zamiilah*
collision تصادم/حادث *tasaadum/haadith*
cologne عطر *`itr*
color لون *lawn*
colored/colorful ملون *mulaw-wan*
comb (n.) مشط *musht*
comb (v.) مشط *mash-shata*
combine ركّب/يركِّب/ركِّب *rak-kaba/yurakkib/rakkib*
combination تركيبة *tarkiibah*
come تعال *ta`aala*
come back ارجع *irji`*
compartment مقصورة (جناح) *maqsuura (janaah)*
complaint شكوى *shakwaa*
complete كامل/إكمال *kaamil/ikmaal*
complement تكملة *takmilah*
compliment مجاملة *mujaamalah*
compliment (v.) جامل/يجامل *jaamala/yujaamil*
computer حاسوب/كمبيوتر *kambyuutar/haasuub*

concert حفلة موسيقية *hafla muusiiqiyya*
concert hall قاعة غناء *qaa`at ghinaa'*
concierge كونسييرج/حارس/بواب *concierge/haaris/baw-waab*
concussion رجة *raj-jah*
condensed milk حليب مكثف *haliib mukath-thaf*
condom غطاء مطاطي *ghitaa' mattaatii*
confectionery حلويات *halawiyyaat*
congratulations تهانينا/مبروك *tahaaniinaa/mabruuk*
connection (transport) رحلة متممة *rihla mutammima*
constipation إمساك *imsaak*
consulate قنصلية *qunsuliyyah*
consultation (by doctor) استشارة *istishaara*
contact lens عدسات *`adasaat*
contagious معدي *mu`dii*
contamination عدوى *`adwaa*
contraceptive pill حبوب منع الحمل *hubuub man` al-haml*
cook (person) طباخ *tabbakh*
cook (v.) طبخ/يطبخ *tabakha/ yatbukh*
cookie بسكويت *baskawiit*
copper (color) نحاسي *nuhaasii*
copy نسخة *nuskha*
copy (v.) نسخ/ينسخ *nasakha/ yansakhu*
corkscrew مفتاح/مبرم *miftaah/ mibraam*
corner ركن *rukn*
cornflower دقيق الذرة *daqiiq adh-dhurah*
correct صحيح *sahiih*
correction تصحيح *tas-hiih*
correspond يراسل *yuraasil*
correspondence مراسلة *muraasalah*
corridor ممر *mamar*
cosmetics مواد تجميل *mawaad tajmiil*
costume زي *zay*
cot سرير طفل *sariir tifl*
cotton قطن *qutn*
cotton wool قطن صوفي *qutn suufiy*
cough سعال/كحة *su`aal/kahha*
cough (v.) يسعل/يكح *yas`ul (yakuh)*
cough syrup شراب كحة *sharaab kahha*
counter عكس/ضد *`aks/did*
country (nation) بلد *balad*
country (rural area) ريف *riif*
country code الترقيم البريدي للبلد *at-tarqiim al-bariidii lil-balad*
courgette كوسا *kuusa*
course of treatment فترة العلاج *fatrat `ilaaj*
cousin بنت خالة/ابن خالة/بنت خال/ابن خالة/بنت عمة/ابن عمة/ بنت عم/ابن عم *ibn `am (f.)/ bint `amm/ibn `ammah/bint `ammah/ibn khaal/bint khaal/ ibn khaalah/bint khaalah*
crab سرطان البحر *arataan al-bahr*
cracker كسارة *kassaara*
cream قشطة *qishta*

credit card بطاقة اعتماد/بطاقة مصرفية *biṯaaqat i`timaad/ biṯaaqa maṣrifiyyah*
crime جريمة *jariimah*
crockery أدوات فخارية *adawaat fak͟hariyya*
cross (road, river) تقاطع *taqaaṯu`*
crossroad تقاطع طرق *taqaaṯu` ṯuruq*
crutch عكاز *`ukkaaz*
cry البكاء *al-bukaa'*
cry (v.) يبكي *yabkii*
cubic meter متر مكعب *mitr muka`ab*
cucumber خيار *k͟hiyaar*
cuddly toy لعبة مسلية *lu`ba musalliya*
cuff الكم *al-kumm*
cufflinks زر كم القميص *zirr kum al-qamiis*
cup كوب/فنجان *kuub/finjaan*
curly (hair) شعر مجعد *sha`r muja`ad*
current (electric) تيار *tayyaar*
curtains ستائر *sataa'ir*
cushion وسادة *wisaada*
custom عادة *`aada*
customs جمارك *jamaarik*
cut (injury) جرح *jurḫ*
cut (v.) يقطع *yaqta`*
cutlery لوازم المائدة *lawaazim al-maa'ida*
cycling ركوب الدرجة *rukuub ad-darraajaa*
cycles دورات *dawraat*

D
dairy products لبنيات *labaniyyaat*
damage ضرر *ḏarar*
dance (n.) رقص *raqṣ*
dance (v.) يرقص *yarquṣ*
dandruff قشرة (شعر) *qis͟hrat (sha`r)*
danger خطر *k͟haṯar*
dangerous خطير *k͟haṯiir*
dark ظلام *ẕalaam*
date تاريخ *taariik͟h*
date of birth تاريخ ميلاد *taariik͟h miilaad*
date(s) تمر *tamr*
daughter بنت *bint*
day يوم *yawm*
day after tomorrow بعد غد *ba`da g͟had*
day before yesterday أول أمس *'awal' ams*
dead ميت *may-yit*
deadly قاتل *qaatil*
deaf أطرش *aṯras͟h*
decaffeinated خالي من الكافيين *k͟haalin min al-kaafiin*
December ديسمبر/كانون الثاني *kaanuun at͟h-t͟haanii/diisember*
declare (customs) يسرح *yusarriḫ*
deep عميق *`amiiq*
deep-freeze تجمد عميق *tajammud `amiiq*
deep-sea diving الغوص في أعماق البحار *al-g͟hawṣ fii 'a`maaq al-biḫaar*

defecate يتغوط *yataghawwat*
degree درجة *darajah*
delay تأخير *ta'khiir*
delicious لذيذ *ladhiidh*
dentist طبيب أسنان *tabiib asnaan*
dentures طقم أسنان *taqm asnaan*
deodorant معطر *mu`attir*
department store محل تجاري *mahall tijaarii*
departure مغادرة *mughaadara*
departure time وقت المغادرة *waqt al-mughaadara*
depilatory cream مستحضر مزيل الشعر *mustahdar muziil lish-sha`r*
deposit (for safekeeping) أمانة/وديعة *amaanah/wadii`ah*
deposit (in bank) يودع *yuudi`*
depot مستودع *mustawda`*
desert صحراء *sahraa'*
dessert حلويات *halawiyyaat*
destination مسيرة/مقصد *masiirah/maqsad*
detergent مادة منظفة *maaddah munaz-zifah*
develop (photo) تحميض *tahmiid*
develop (make something) تطوير/إنشاء *tatwiir/inshaa'*
diabetes داء السكري *daa' as-suk-kariy*
diabetic مريض بداء السكري *mariid bidaa' as-suk-kariy*
dial طلب رقم على الهاتف *talab raqm `alaa al-haatif*
diamond الماس *almas*
diaper حفاظ الطفل *haffad tifl*
diarrhea إسهال *'is-haal*
dictionary قاموس *qaamuus*
diesel oil زيت الديزل *zayt ad-diizil*
diet (food) غذاء *ghidhaa'*
diet (regime) حمية *himyah*
difficult صعب *sa`b*
difficulty صعوبة *su`uubah*
dine (v.) يأكل *ya'kul*
dining car عربة طعام *`arabat ta`aam*
dining room غرفة الطعام/غرفة الأكل *ghurfat at-ta`aam/ ghurfatu al'akl*
dinner عشاء *`ashaa'*
direct (n.) مباشر *mubaashar*
direct (v.) يوجه *yuwajih*
direct flight طيران مباشر *tayaraan mubaashar*
direction اتجاه *ittijaah*
directly مباشرة *mubaasharatan*
dirt (n.) وسخ/تراب *wasakh/ turaab*
dirty وسخ *wasikh*
disabled معاق *mu`aaq*
disco ديسكو *diskuu*
discount تخفيض *takhfiid*
dish صحن *sahn*
dish (food) طبق *tabaq*
dish of the day طبق اليوم *tabaq al-yawm*
disinfect (v.) تطهير *tat-hiir*
disinfectant مطهر *mutah-hir*
distance مسافة *masaafah*
distill تقطير *taqtiir*

distilled water ماء مقطر *maa' muqattar*
disturb يزعج *yuz`ij*
disturbance إزعاج *iz`aaj*
dive يغوص *yaghuus*
diver غطاس *ghat-taas*
diving غطس *ghats*
diving board منصة الغوص *manassat al-ghaws*
diving gear لوازم الغوص *lawaazim al-ghaws*
divorce طلاق *talaaq*
divorced مطلق *mutal-laq*
divorced (v.) مطلقة *mutal-laqah*
dizzy دوار *duwaar*
do اعمل *'a`mal*
do (v.) عمل *`amila*
doctor طبيب/طبيبة *tabiib/tabiibah* (f.)
dog كلب *kalb*
do-it-yourself store محل خدمات ذاتية *mahal khadamaat dhaatiyya*
doll دمية *dumiya*
dome قبة *qubbah*
domestic محلي *mahallii*
done (cooked) مطبوخ *matbuukh*
do not disturb الرجاء عدم الإزعاج *ar-rajaa' `adam al-iz`aaj*
door باب *baab*
doormat ممسحة *mamsaha*
dormant نائم *naai'm*
dormitory عمبر النوم *`anbar an-nawam*
double ضعف *di`f*
down أسفل *asfal*
download تحميل *tahmiil*
drapes ستائر *sataa'ir*
draught جفاف *jafaaf*
dream (v.) يحلم *yahlum*
dream (n.) حلم *hulum*
dress يلبس *yalbas*
dress (n.) فستان *fustaan*
dressing gown عباءة *`abaa'a*
drink (v.) يشرب *yashrab*
drink (refreshment) شراب/مشروب *sharaab/mashruub*
drinking water ماء شرب *maa' shrub*
drive يسوق *yasuuq*
driver سائق *saa'iq*
driver's license رخصة سياقة *rukhsat siyaaqa*
drugstore مخزن أدوية *makhzan adwiya*
drunk سكران *sakraan*
dry جاف *jaaf*
dry (v.) يجف/يجف *yujaff/yajuff*
dry-clean غسل على الجاف *ghasl `ala-aljaaf*
drycleaners دراي كلينرز *dray kliiners*
duck بطة *bat-taah*
duck (head) وطى *wat-taa*
during خلال/أثناء *khilaal/athnaa'*
during the day خلال اليوم *khilaal al-yawm*
duty (tax) رسم جمركي *rasm jumrukiy*
duty-free (goods) بضاعة غير خاضعة للرسم الجمركي *bidaa`ah ghayr khaadi`ah lir-rasm al-jumrukiy*

duty-free shop دكان معفى من الرسوم *dukaan mu`faa mina ar-rusuum*
DVD دي في دي *dii fii dii*

E

ear أذن *udhun*
earache ألم/وجع في الأذن *'alam/waja` fii al-udhun*
ear drops قطر للأذن *qatra lil–udhun*
early مبكر *mubakkir*
earphone سماعة *samaa`ah*
earrings أقراط *aqrat*
earth أرض *ard*
earthenware خزف *khazaf*
ease سهولة *suhuulah*
east شرق *sharq*
Easter عيد الفصح *Eiid al fush*
eastern شرقية *sharqiyah*
easy سهل *sahl*
eat (v.) أكل *akala*
economics الاقتصاد *al-iqtisaad*
economist خبير اقتصادي *khabiir iqtisaadiy*
economy اقتصاد *iqtisaad*
economy class درجة اقتصادية *daraja iqtisaadiyya*
eczema أكزمة *akzima*
eel (سمكة) الانقليص/الجريش *(samakat) al-anqaliis/aljariith*
egg بيض *bayd*
eggplant باذنجان *baadhinjaan*
electric كهرباء *kahrabaa'ii*
electrical كهربائية *kahrubaaiyyah*
electrician كهربائي *kahrabaa'iy*
electricity كهربائي *kahrabaa'*
electronic إلكتروني *ilikituunii*
elephant فيل *fiil*
elevate رفع *rafa`*
elevator مصعد كهربائي *mis`ad kahrabaa'iy*
email بريد إلكتروني *bariid iliktoronii*
embassy سفارة *sifaarah*
emergency حالة طوارئ *haalat tawaari'*
emergency brake مكابح طوارئ *makaabih tawaari'*
emergency exit مخرج طوارئ *makhraj tawaari'*
emergency phone هاتف طوارئ *haatif tawaari'*
emergency room غرفة الطوارئ/الاستعجالات *ghurfat at-tawari'/alisti`jalaat*
emperor إمبراطور *imbiraatuur*
empire إمبراطورية *ambraturiyyah*
empress امبراطورة *imbiraatuura*
emptiness فراغ *faraagh*
empty فارغ *faarigh/shaaghir*
engaged (on the phone) مشغول *mashghuul*
engaged (to be married) مخطوب/مخطوبة *makhtuub/* (f.) *makhtuuba*
engagement خطوبة *khutuuba*
England إنجلترا *inglitaraa*
English إنجليزي *ingliiziy*
English (f.) إنجليزية *ingliiziy-yah*
enjoy تمتع *tamat-ta`*
enquire يستفسر/تساءل *yastafsir/tasaa'l*

enquiry استفسار *istifsaar*
envelope ظرف *zarf*
escalator درج ميكانيكي *daraj miikaaniikii*
escort رافق/مرافق *raafiq/muraafiq*
essence جوهر/أساس *jawhar/asaas*
essential أساسي *asaasii*
evening مساء *masaa'*
evening wear لباس المساء *libaas al-masaa'*
event حدث/مناسبة *hadath/munaasaba*
ever في أي وقت *fi ayi waqt*
every كل *kull*
everything كل شيء *kull shay'*
everywhere كل مكان *kull makaan*
examine يفحص *yafhas*
excavation حفر/تنقيب *hafr/tanqiib*
excellency سعادة *sa`aadet*
excellent ممتاز *mumtaaz*
exchange يصرف عملة *yusarrif `umlah*
exchange office مكتب تصريف *maktab tasriif*
excursion رحلة *rihla*
exhibit معرض *ma`rad*
exhibition عرض *`arad*
exit مخرج *makhraj*
exit (v.) خرج *kharaja*
expand توسيع *tawsii`*
expand (time) تمديد *tamdiid*
expenses مصاريف/نفاقات *masaariif/nafaqaat*
expensive غالي *ghaalin*
explain يشرح *yashrah*
express عبر *`ab-bar*
external خارجي *khaarijii*
eye عين *`ayn*
eyebrow(s) حاجب/حواجب *haajib/hawaajib*
eye drop قطر للعين *qatra lil-`ayn*
eyelash رمش العين *ramsh al`ayn*
eye specialist أخصائي عيون *akhissaa'ii `uyuun*

F

fabric قماش *qumaash*
face وجه *wajh*
Facebook فيسبوك *Fiisbuuk*
factory مصنع *masna`*
fall (season) خريف *khariif*
fall (v.) يسقط *yasqut*
family عائلة *`aa'ila*
famous مشهور *mashhuur*
fan مروحة *mirwahah*
far away بعيد *ba`iid*
farm مزرعة *mazra`ah*
farmer فلاح/مزارع *muzaari`/fallah*
fashion زي *zay*
fast سريع *sari`*
father أب *'ab*
father-in-law الحمو *al-hamuw*
fault خطأ *khata'*
fax فاكس *faaks*
February شباط/فبراير *febraayar/shubaat*
feel يشعر *yash`ur*

feel like ود *wad-da*
feelings مشاعر *mashaai`r*
fence سور *suur*
ferry سفينة/عبارة *`ab-baara / safiina*
fever حمى/حرارة *haraarah/ hum-maa*
feverish محموم/ساخن *mahmuum/saakhin*
fiancé خطيب *khatiib*
fiancée (f.) خطيبة *khatiibah*
fill يملأ *yamla'*
filling (dental) حشوة *hashwa*
filling (in food) حشو *hashw*
fill out (form) يملأ *yamla'*
film (cinema; photo) فيلم *film*
filter مصفاة *misfaat (filtar)*
filter cigarette فلتر سيجارة *filtar sijaara*
fine (good) جيد/حسن *hasan/ jay-yid*
fine (money) غرامة/خطية *gharaama/khatiyya*
finger إصبع *isba`*
fire نار/حريق *naar/hariiq*
fire alarm منبه حريق *munabbih hariiq*
fire department المطافئ *al-mataafi'*
fire escape مهرب حريق *mahrab hariiq*
fire extinguisher آلة اطفاء النار *aalat itfaa' an-naar*
first أول *awwal*
first (f.) أولى *'uulaa*
first aid إسعافات أولية *is`aafaat awwaliyya*
first class درجة أولى *daraja 'uulaa*
fish سمكة/سمك *samakah/samak*
fish (v.) اصطاد (السمك) *istaada (as-samak)*
fishing اصطياد (السمك) *istiyaaad (as-samak)*
fishing rod عصا الصيد *`asaa as-sayd*
fit صالح/مناسب *saalih/munaasib*
fitness لياقة بدنية *liyaaqa badaniyyah*
fitness club نادي لياقة *naadii liyaaqa*
fitness training تدريب لياقة *tadriib liyaaqa*
fitting room غرفة القياس *ghurfat al-qiyaas*
fix (puncture) أصلح *uslih*
flag علم *`alam*
flash (camera) ضوء *daw' (flash)*
flashlight مصباح يدوي *misbah yadawiy*
flat مسطح *mosat-tah*
flat (apartment) شقة *shuqqa*
flatulence تطبيل/نفخ *tatbiil/nafkh*
flavor نكهة *nakha*
flavoring مادة منهكة *maadda munakkiha*
flea برغوث *barghuuth*
flea market سوق البرغوث/ الخردوات *suuq al-barghuuth/ alkhardawaat*
flight رحلة (طيران) *rihlat (tayaraan)*

flight number رقم الرحلة *raqam ar-rihla*
flood فيضان *fayadaan*
floor (ground) أرضية *ardiyya*
floor (storey) طابق *taabiq*
flour طحين *tahiin*
flower زهرة *zahra*
flu الإنفلونزا *al-influwanza*
flush (v.) يغسل *yaghsil*
fly (insect) ذبابة *dhubaaba*
fly (v.) يطير *yatiir*
fog ضباب *dabaab*
foggy ضبابي *dabaabii*
folklore فولكلور *fuliklor*
follow يتبع *yatba`*
food (groceries) مواد غذائية *mawaad ghidhaa'iyya*
food (meal) طعام (غذاء) *ta`aam (ghidhaa')*
food court ساحة مطاعم *saahat mataa`im*
food poisoning تسمم غذائي *tasammum ghidhaa'ii*
foot قدم *'qadam*
foot brake فرامل/ مكبح القدم *faramil/mikbah al-qadam*
forbidden ممنوع *mamuu`*
forbidden (more emphatic) محرم *muhar-ram*
forbid (v.) يمنع *yamna`*
forehead جبين *jabiin*
foreign غريب/أجنبي *ghariib/ajnabii*
forget ينسى *yansaa*
fork شوكة *shawka*
form استمارة *istimaara*
formal dress زي رسمي *zay rasmii*
forward (letter) يرسل *yursil*
fountain نافورة *nafuurah*
frame إطار *itaar*
free حر *hur*
free (unoccupied) شاغر *shaaghir*
free (no charge) مجاني *majjaanii*
free time وقت فراغ *waqt faraagh*
freeze تجميد *tajmiid*
freezer براد *barraad*
French fries بطاطس مقلية *bataatis maqliyyah*
fresh طازج *taazaj*
Friday الجمعة *Al-jumu`a*
fried مقلي *maqlii*
friend صديق *sadiiq*
friendly ودي *widdii*
frighten مذعور/مذعورة *madh`uur/madh`uurah* (f.)
fringe (hair) القصةُ *al-qussa*
frozen مجمد *mujammad*
fruit فواكه *fawaakih*
fruit juice عصير فواكه *`asiir fawaaqih*
fry قلى/يقلي *qalaa/yaqlii*
full شبعان/مملوء *shab`aan/mamluu'*
fun مرح/لهو *marah/lahw*
funeral جنازة *janazah*
funny مضحك *mud-hik*

G

gallery بهو (صالة) *bahw (saala)*
game لعبة *lu`ba*
garage (car repair) ورشة تصليح *warshat tasliih*

garbage قمامة/نفايات *qomaama/ nifaayaat*
garden حديقة *hadiiqa*
garlic ثوم *thuum*
garment ثوب *thawb*
gas (for heating) غاز *ghaaz*
gas station محطة وقود *mahat-tat waquud*
gasoline بنزين *banziin*
gate بوابة *bawwaaba*
gear (car) الطروس *at-turuus*
gem جوهرة *jawhara*
gender الجنس *al-jins*
get off يخرج/ينزل *yakhruj/yanzil*
get on يصعد *yas`ad*
gift هدية *hadiyya*
ginger زنجبيل *zanjabiil*
girl بنت *bint*
girlfriend صديقة *sadiiqa*
given name الاسم *al-ism*
glass (for drinking) كوب/كأس *kuub/ka's*
glass (material) زجاج *zujaaj*
glasses النظارات *enazzaaraat*
gliding طيران شراعي *tayaraan shiraa`ii*
Global Positioning System (GPS) نظام تحديد المواقع العالمي (جي بي اس) *Nizaam Tahdiid Al-mawaqi` Al-`alamii (jii bii as)*
glossy (photo) لامع *laami`*
gloves قفازات *quffaazaat*
glue صمغ *samagh*
go اذهب *idhhab*
go back ارجع *irji`*
go out اخرج *ukhruj*
gold ذهب *dhahab*
golden ذهبي *dhahabiy*
golf جولف/صولجان *gulf/ sawlajaan*
golf course ملعب الجولف *mal`ab al-gulf*
good afternoon مساء الخير *massa' al-khayr*
good evening مساء الخير *massa' al-khayr*
good morning صباح الخير *sabaah al-khayr*
good night تصبح على خير *tusbih `alaa khayr*
goodbye مع السلامة *ma'a as-salaama*
goose إوزة *iwazza*
gram غرام *ghraam*
grandchild حفيد *hafiid*
granddaughter حفيدة *hafiida*
grandfather جد *jad*
grandmother جدة *jadda*
grandparents الجدان *al-jad-daan*
grandson حفيد *hafiid*
grape juice عصير عنب *`asiir `inab*
grapes عنب *`inab*
grave قبر *qabr*
graveyard مقبرة *maqbara*
gray رمادي *ramaadii*
gray-haired ذو شعر رمادي *dhuu sha'r ramaadii*
graze يرعى *yar`aa*
grease شحم *shahm*
greasy مشحم *mushah-ham*
green أخضر *akhdar*

greenery المساحات الخضراء *al masaahaat al khadraa'*
greengrocer خضار *khad-dar*
greens الخضار *al khudaar*
greet يحيي *yuhayii*
greeting تحية *tahiyya*
grilled مشوي *mashwii*
groceries بقالة *biqaala*
group مجموعة *majmuu`a*
guest house بيت ضيافة *bayt diyaafa*
guide (book) دليل *daliil*
guide (person) موجه/مرشد *muwajjih/murshid*
guided tour رحلة مع مرشد *rihla ma`a murshid*
guilt ذنب/إثم *dhanb/ithm*
guilty مذنب/آثم *mudhnib/aathim*
gym جمناستك *jumnaastik*
gym (club) نادي رياضي *naadii riyaaidiy*
gym (school) حصة رياضة *his-sat riyaadah*
gymnastics الجمباز *al-jimbaaz*
gynecologist أخصائي أمراض النساء *akhissaii amraad an-nisaa'*

H

hair شعر *sha`r*
hairbrush مشط *misht*
haircut قصة شعر *qassat sha`r*
hairdresser حلاق/حلاقة *hallaaq/hallaaqah* (f.)
hairdryer مجفف شعر *mujaffif sha`r*
hairspray رشاش شعر *rashaash sha`r*
hairstyle تسريح شعر *tasriihat sha`r*
half نصف *nisf*
half full نصف مملوء *nisf mamluu'*
hammer مطرقة *mitraqa*
hand يد *yad*
hand brake فرامل يدوية *fraamil yadawiyya*
hand luggage حقيبة يد *haqiiba yad*
hand towel منشفة *minshafa*
handbag حقيبة يد *haqiibat yad*
handkerchief منديل *mindiil*
handmade صنع يدوي *sun`yadawii*
happy سعيد *sa`iid*
harbor ميناء *minaa'*
hard (difficult) صعب *sa`b*
hard (firm) صلب/قاسي *salb/qaasii*
hardware store متجر مواد معدنية *matjar mawaad ma`daniyya*
hat قبعة *qubba`a*
hay fever حمى القش *humma al-qash*
head رأس *ra's*
headache صداع *sudaa`*
headlights إضاءة أمامية *idaa'a amaamiyya*
heal يشفي *yashfii*
healing شفاء *shifaa'*
health صحة *sihhaa*
health food shop دكان أطعمة صحية *dukkaan at`ima sihhiyya*
healthy صحي *sihhii*

hear يسمع *yasma`*
hearing aid سماعة أذن *sammaa`aat udhun*
heart قلب *qalb*
heart attack أزمة قلبية *azma qalbiyya*
heat تدفئة *tadfiah*
heater مدفأة *midfa'a*
heating system جهاز تدفئة *jihaaz tafi'ah*
heavy ثقيل *thaqiil*
heel (of foot) كعب *ka`b*
he (pron.) هو *huwa*
Hello أهلاً *Ahlan*
help مساعدة/النجدة *musaa`ada/ an-najda*
helping (of food) معونة *ma`uuna*
hem حافة *haaffah*
her هي *hia*
herb عشب *`ushb*
herbal tea شاي الأعشاب *shaay al-aa`shaab*
here هنا *hunaa*
high عالي *`aalii*
high chair كرسي للأطفال *kursii lil-atfaal*
high tide أعلى مستوى للمد *a`laa mustawaa lil-mad*
highway طريق سريع *tariiq sari`*
hiking نزهة سير على الأقدام *nuzhat sayr `alaa al-aqdaam*
hiking boots حذاء نزهات السير على الأقدام *hidhaa' nuzhat as-sayr `alaa al-aqdaam*
hip ورك *wirk*
hire يستأجر *yasta'jir*
hitchhike سفر تطفلي *safar tataffulii*
hobby هواية *hiwaaya*
hold up سرقة/توقف *sariqah/ tawaqquf*
holiday (festival) مهرجان *mahrajaan*
holiday (public) عطلة *`utlah*
holiday (vacation) إجازة *ijaaza*
homesick الحنين إلى الوطن *al-haniin ilal-watan*
honest أمين *amiin*
honey عسل *`asal*
horizon الأفق *al'ufuq*
horizontal أفقي *'ufuqii*
horrible كريه *kariih*
horse حصان *hisaan*
hospital مستشفى *mustashfaa*
hospitality ضيافة *diyaafa*
hot (bitter, sharp) حاد *haad*
hot (warm) حار *haar*
hot spring ينبوع ساخن *yanbu` sakhin*
hot-water bottle زجاجة ماء ساخن *zujaajat maa' saakhin*
hotel فندق *funduq*
hour ساعة *saa`a*
house بيت *bayt*
houses of parliament مقر البرلمان *maqar al-barlamaan*
How? كيف؟ *Kayf?*
How far? كم المسافة؟ *Kam al-masaafa?*
How long? كم المدة؟ *Kam al-mudda?*

How many? كم/كم عدد؟ *Kam/ kam `adad?*
How much? (price) بكم؟ *Bikam?*
hundred مئة *mi'a*
hundred grams مئة غرام *mi'at ghraam*
hungry جائع/ جوعان *(m) jaa'i`/ jaw`aan*
hunt يصطاد/يتابع *yastaad/ yutaabi`*
hurry أسرع/بسرعة *asri`/bisur`a*
hurt يؤلم *yu'lim*
husband زوج *zawj*
hut كوخ *kuukh*

I

ice جليد *jaleed*
ice cream بوظة *buuda*
ice cubes مكعبات ثلج *muka`abaat thalj*
iced مثلج *muthallaj*
ice-skating تزلج على الثلج/الجليد *tazalluj `alaa ath-thalj/aljaleed*
idea فكرة *fikra*
identification (card) بطاقة شخصية *bitaaqa shakhsiyya*
identify يتعرف *yuta`arraf*
identity هوية *hawiya*
ignition key مفتاح قدح *miftaah qadh*
ill مريض *mariid*
illness مرض *marad*
imagination الخيال *al khayal*
imagine يتخيل *yatakhayyal*
immediately حالاً *haalan*
import (v.) استيراد *istiiraad*
import duty ضريبة الاستيراد *dariibat al-istiiraad*
important مهم *muhim*
impossible مستحيل *mustahiil*
improve يطور/يحسن *yutawwir/ yuhassin*
in في الداخل *fid-daakhil*
in the evening في المساء *fii al-masaa'*
in the morning في الصباح *fii as-sabaah*
indigestion سوء هضم *suu' hadm*
in-laws الأنساب *al-ansaab*
included مشمول *mashmuul*
include in يشمل *yashmal*
indicate يوضح *yuwaddih*
indicator (car) إشارة *ishaara*
inexpensive رخيص *rakhiis*
infect يعدي *ya`dii*
infection إلتهاب/ عدوى *Iltihaab/`adwaa*
infectious معدي *mu`dii*
inflame يلتهب *yaltahib*
inflammation التهاب *iltihaab*
inform يعلم *yu`lim*
information معلومات *ma`luumaat*
information office مكتب المعلومات *maktab al-ma`luumaat*
inject حقن *haqn*
injection حقنة *huqna*
injure يصيب *yusiib*
injured مصاب *musaab*
injury إصابة *isaabah*
ink حبر *hibr*
inn نزل *nazl*

innocent بريء *barii'*
innocence براءة *baraa'ah*
insect حشرة *hasharah*
insect bite لدغة حشرة *ladghat hasharah*
insert إدراج *idraaj*
inside داخل *daakhil*
install تركيب *tarkiib*
installation تثبيت *tathbiit*
instruct إرشاد *irshaad*
instructions تعليمات *ta`liimaat*
insurance الضمان/التأمين *addamaan/at-ta'miin*
insure تؤمن *tu'amiin*
interfere يتدخل *yatadakh-khal*
interference تدخل *tadakhul*
intermission فترة استراحة *fatrat istiraaha*
intern متدرب *mutadarrib*
internal داخلي *daakhilii*
international دولي *duwalii*
Internet إنترنت/شبكة الإنترنت *Internet/shabakatul Internet*
Internet café (cyber) مقهى إنترنت (سايبر) *maqha Internet (saybar)*
internship تدريب داخلي *tadriib (daakhiliy)*
interpret ترجم/فسر *tarjama/ fas-sara*
interpretation ترجمة *tarjamah*
interpreter مترجم/مفسر *mutarjim/mufassir*
intersect يقطع *yaqta`*
intersection تقاطع *taqaatu`*
introduce تقديم *taqdiim*
introduce oneself يقدم (يعرف) *yuqaddim (yu`arrif)*
introduction مقدمة/تعريف *muqadimah/ta`riif*
invitation دعوة *da`wah*
invite يدعو *yad`uu*
invoice فاتورة *faatuura*
iodine اليود *al-yuud*
Ireland إيرلندا *irlandaa*
Irish إيرلندي *irlandiy*
Irish (f.) إيرلندية *irlandiy-yah*
iron (metal) حديد *hadiid*
iron (clothes) مكواة *mikwaat*
iron (v.) يكوي *yakwii*
ironing board *lawh kawii*
island جزيرة *jaziirah*
itch حكة *hakkah*
itch (v.) حك *hak-ka*

J

jack (for car) رافعة *raafi`a*
jacket جاكيت/سترة *jaakiit (sutra)*
jam مربى *murab-baa*
January كانون الثاني/يناير *yanaayar/kanuun aththaanii*
jaw فك *fak*
jeans جينز *jeanz*
jelly جيلي *jalii*
jellyfish قنديل البحر *qindiil al-bahr*
jewel جوهرة *jawharah*
jeweler صائغ *saa'igh*
jewelry مجوهرات *mujawharaat*
jewels جواهر *jawaahir*
job شغل/وظيفة *shughl/waziifa*
jobless عاطل عن العمل *`aati `an al`amal*
jog ركض *rakd*

jog (v.) رَكض *rakada*
joke نكتة *nukta*
joke (v.) نكت *nak-kata*
journey رحلة *rihla*
journey (v.) رحل *rahala*
juice عصير *`asiir*
July تموز/يوليو *Tammuuz/Yulyu*
June حزيران/يونيو *Huzayraan/ Yunyuu*
junk خردة *khurda*
junk food وجبات غير صحية *wajbat ghayr sihiyya*
junk mail بريد غير مرغوب فيه *bariid ghiir marghoub fiih*

K
kerosene كيروسين *kiirusiin*
key مفتاح *miftaah*
keychain/key ring سلسلة مفاتيح *silsilatu mafatiih*
kid طفل *tifl*
kidney الكلية *al-kilya*
kilogram كيلوغرام *kiloghraam*
king ملك *malik*
kiss قبلة *qubla*
kiss (v.) قبّل/يُقبّل *qabbala/ yuqabbil*
kitchen مطبخ *matbakh*
knee ركبة *rukba*
knife سكين *sikiin*
knit يحوك *yahuuk*
know عرف/يعرف *`arafa/ya`rif*
known معروف *ma`ruuf*

L
lace (fabric) زخرفة *zakhrafa*
laces (for shoes) رباط الحذاء *ribaata al-hidhaa'*
lad فتى *fataa*
ladder سلّم *sul-lam*
lake بحيرة *buhayra*
lamb خروف (حمل) *kharuuf (hamal)*
lamp مصباح *misbaah*
land (ground) أرض *'ard*
land (plane) تحط (تنزل) *tahut (tanzil)*
lane (of traffic) مسار *masaar*
language لغة *lugha*
laptop حاسوب محمول *hasoub mahmoul*
large كبير/واسع *kabiir (waasi`)*
last (endure) يستمر *yastamir*
last (final) آخر *aakhir*
last night الليلة الماضية *al-layla al-maadiya*
late متأخر *muta'akhir*
later فيما بعد *fiimaa ba`d*
laugh يضحك *yad-hak*
launder غسل *ghasl*
laundrette مؤسسة غسل و كوي *mu'assasat ghasl wa kawii*
laundromat مغسلة *maghsalah*
laundry غسيل *ghasiil*
laundry soap صابون ملابس *saabun malaabis*
law قانون *qaanuun*
lawyer محامي *muhaamii*
laxative مسهل (ملين) *musahil (mulayyin)*
leak تسرب *tasarrub*
leather جلد *jild*

leather goods بضاعة جلدية *bidaa`ah jildiyya*
leave غادر/يغادر *ghaadar/yughaadir*
left (residual) متبقي *mutabaqqii*
left (hand) يسار *yasaar*
leg ساق *saaq*
leggings غطاء الساقين *ghitaa' as-saaqayn*
leisure وقت فراغ *waqt faragh*
lemon ليمون *laymuun*
lend يقرض *yuqrid*
lens (camera) عدسات *`adasaat*
less أقل *aqal*
lesson درس *dars*
letter (mail) رسالة *risaala*
letter (alphabet) حرف *harf*
lettuce خص *khass*
level crossing معبر *ma`bar*
library مكتبة *maktaba*
license رخصة/إجازة *rukhsa/ijaaza*
lie (v.) كذب *kadhaba*
lie (falsehood) كذب *kadhib*
lie down يستلقي *yastalqii*
lift (elevator) مصعد *mis`ad*
lift (in car) توصيلة *tawsiila*
lift رفع *raf`*
light (lamp) مصباح *misbaah*
light (not dark) ضوء *daw`*
light (not heavy) خفيف *khafiif*
light bulb مصباح *misbaah*
lighter قداحة *qiddaha*
lightning البرق *al-barq*
like (v.) يحب (يرغب)/أحب (رغب) *yuhib (yarghab)/ahab-ba (raghiba)*
line خط *khat*
linen كتان *kittaan*
lining بطانة *bitaana*
listen سمع/أصغى *'asaghaa/sami`a*
liter لتر *litr*
literature آداب *adaab*
litter قمامة *qumaamah*
little (amount) قليل *qaliil*
little (small) صغير *saghiir*
live (alive) يعيش/عاش *ya`iish/`aasha*
live (v.) يسكن *yaskun*
liver الكبد *al-kabid*
lobster جراد البحر *jaraad al-bahr*
local محلي *mahallii*
location موقع/منطقة *mawqi`/mantiqah*
lock قفل *qufl*
lock (v.) يقفل/قفل *yaqfil/qafala*
long طويل *tawiil*
long-distance call مكالمة بعيدة *maukaalama ba`iida*
look at ينظر إلى *yanzur 'ilaa*
look for يبحث عن/بحث عن *yabhath `an/bahatha `an*
look up يبحث عن/بحث عن *yabhath `an/bahatha*
loose فضفاض/فضفاضة *fdfaadah (f) fdfaad*
lose يفقد/فقد *yafqid/faqada*
loss خسارة (فقدان) *khasaara (fiqdaan)*
lost (can't find way) مفقود *mafquud'*
lost (missing) ضائع *daa'i`*

lost and found office مكتب الموجودات و المفقودات *maktab al-mawjuudaat wa al-mafquudaat*
lotion محلول *mahlul*
loud عالي *'aaliy*
love حب *hub*
love (v.) يحب/أحب *yuhib/ahab-ba*
low منخفض *munkhafid*
low tide أدنى مستوى للجزر *adnaa mustawaa lil-jazr*
LPG غاز *ghaz*
luck حظ *haz*
luggage أمتعة/حقائب *amti`ah/haqaa'ib*
luggage locker خزانة الحقائب *khizaanat al-haqaa'ib*
lumps (sugar) قطع سكر *qita` suk-kar*
lumps كتل *kutal*
lunch غداء *ghadaa'*
lungs الرئتان *ar-ri'ataan*

M

madam مدام (سيدة) *madam (sayyida)*
magazine مجلة *majalla*
mail (letters) بريد *bariid*
mail (v.) يرسل/أرسل بالبريد *yursil/arsala bilbariid*
main post office مكتب البريد الرئيسي *maktab al-briid ar-ra'iisii*
main road طريق رئيسي *tariiq ra'iisii*
make, create يصنع/يخلق *yasna`/yakhluq*
make an appointment يحدد موعد *yuhaddid mau`id*
make love يمارس الجنس *yumaaris al-jins*
makeshift بديل مؤقت *badiil mu'aqqat*
makeup مكياج *mikyaaj*
man رجل *rajul*
manage أدار *adaara*
management إدارة *idaarah*
manager مدير *mudiir*
mandate يأمر/أمر *ya'mur/'amara*
mandatory إلزامي *ilzamiy*
mango منجا *mangaa*
manhood الرجولة *ar-rujulah*
manicure صبغ أظافر *subgh azaafir*
manufacture (produce) إنتاج *intaaj*
manufacture (a company) شركة إنتاج *sharikat intaaj*
many كثير *kathiir*
map خارطة *khaarita*
marble مرمر *marmar*
March آذار/مارس *Aadhaar/Maaras*
margarine زبدة/سمن *zubda/samn*
marina مرسى/مارينا *marsaa/maarinah*
marital status الحالة المدنية *al-haala al-madaniyya*
market سوق *suuq*
marriage زواج *zawaaj*
married متزوج *mutazawwij*
marry يتزوج/تزوج *yatazaw-waj/tazaw-waj*
mass كتلة *kutla*

massage تدليك *tadliik*
mat (on floor) سجادة صغيرة/ حصيرة *sijjaada saghiira/ hasiirah*
mat (on table) قطعة قماش الطاولة *qit`at qumaash at-taawila*
match يوافق (يناسب) *yuwaafiq (yunaasib)*
match (sport/game) مباراة *mubaarah*
matches كبريت *kibriit*
May أيار/مايو *Maayuu/Aayaar*
maybe ربما *rubbamaa*
mayonnaise مايونيز *maayuuniiz*
mayor محافظ *muhaafiz*
meal وجبة غذائية *wajba (ghidhaa'iyya)*
mean يعني *ya`nii*
mean (nasty) سيئ *say-yi'*
means (income) دخل *dakhl*
measure يقيس/قاس *yaqiis/qaas*
measure out يقيس *yaqiis*
meat لحم *lahm*
medical طبي *tib-biy*
medication علاج *`ilaaj*
medicine دواء *dawaa'*
meet يلتقي ب *yaltaqii*
melon بطيخ (شمام) *battikh (shammaam)*
member عضو *`udw*
member of parliament عضو البرلمان *`udw barlamaan*
membership card بطاقة عضوية *bitaaqat `udwiyya*
mend يصلح/تصليح *yuslih/tasliih*
menstruation حيض *hayd*
menu قائمة المأكولات *qaa'imat al-ma'kuulaat*
message رسالة *risaala*
metal معدن *ma`dan*
meter متر *mitr*
meter (in taxi) عداد *`addad*
mice فئران *fi'raan*
migraine صداع/الشقيقة *sudaa`/ ash-shaqiiqa*
mild (taste) لطيف *latiif*
milk حليب *haliib*
millimeter ملمتر *millimitr*
mineral معدني *ma`daniy*
mineral water مياه معدنية *miyaah ma`daniyya*
minute دقيقة *daqiiqa*
mirror مرآة *mir'aat*
mirror (reflect) يعكس *ya`kis*
miss (flight, train) يتأخر عن *yata'akhar `an*
miss (loved one) يشتاق *yashtaaq*
missing مفقود *mafquud*
missing (f.) مفقودة *mafquudah*
missing (person) مفقود *mafquud*
mist ضباب *dabaab*
mistake خطأ/غلط *khata' (ghalat)*
mistaken مخطئ *mukhti'*
mister سيدي/مستر *sayid-di/ mistar*
misty ضبابي *dabaabiy*
misunderstanding سوء فهم *suu' fahm*
mix (blend) مزج/خلط *mazj/khalt*
mixed ممزوج *mamzuuj*
mixture خلطة/خليط *khaltah/ khaliit*

moderate معتدل *mu`tadil*

moderation اعتدال *i`tidal*

modern حديث <u>*hadiith*</u>

modern art الفن الحديث *al-fan al-<u>h</u>adiith*

modernization تحديث *ta<u>h</u>diith*

moment لحظة *la<u>h</u>za*

momentarily عن قريب/قريباً *`an qariib/qariiban*

momentary مؤقت *mo`aqqat*

monastery دير *dayr*

Monday يوم الاثنين *(yawm) a-ithnayn*

monetary نقدية *naqdiy-yah*

money مال/نقود (فلوس) *maal/nuquud (fuluus)*

monkey قرد *qird*

month شهر *shahr*

monthly (f.) شهرياً/شهرية *<u>sh</u>ahriy/<u>sh</u>ahriy-yah*

moon قمر *qamar*

mop مسح *mash*

moped دراجة نارية *dar-raajah naariy-yah*

mosquito بعوضة *baa`uu<u>d</u>ah*

mosquito net شبكة البعوض *<u>sh</u>abakat ba`uud*

motel فندق صغير *funduq <u>sagh</u>iir*

mother أم *um*

motherhood أمومة *umuumah*

mother-in-law الحماة *al-<u>h</u>amaah*

motor محرك *mu<u>h</u>ar-rik*

motorbike دراجة نارية *dar-raajah naariy-yah*

motorboat زورق بمحرك *zawraq bi-mu<u>h</u>arrik*

motorist سائق *saai`q*

mountain جبل *jabal*

mountain hut كوخ جبلي *kuu<u>kh</u> jabalii*

mountainous جبلي/جبلية *jabaliy/ (f.) jabaliy-yah*

mouse فأر *fa`r*

mouth فم/ثغر *fam/<u>thaghr</u>*

MSG رسالة *risaala*

much كثير *kathiir*

mud طين/وحل *wa<u>h</u>l/<u>t</u>iin*

muddy موحل *muuhal*

muscle عضلة *`a<u>d</u>ala*

muscle spasms تقلص عضلي *taqallu<u>s</u> `a<u>d</u>alii*

muscular قوي *qawiy*

museum متحف *mat<u>h</u>af*

mushrooms الفطر *al-fi<u>t</u>r*

music موسيقا *muusiiqaa*

musical موسيقي *musiiqiy*

N

nail (finger) ظفر *<u>z</u>ifr*

nail (metal) مسمار *mismaar*

nail file مبرد أظافر *mibrad a<u>z</u>aafir*

nail scissors مقص أظافر *miqa<u>s</u> a<u>z</u>aafir*

naked عريان/عريانة *`aryaan/`aryaanah (f.)*

nappy, diaper حفاظ طفل *<u>h</u>iffaa<u>z</u> <u>t</u>ifl*

national وطني/وطنية *wa<u>t</u>aniy/ (f.) wa<u>t</u>aniy-yah*

nationality جنسية *jinsiyya*

natural طبيعي *<u>t</u>abii`ii*

nature طبيعة *<u>t</u>abii`a*

nausea غثيان *ghathayaan*
nauseous مقرف *muqrif*
near قرب *qurb*
nearby قريب *qariib*
nearly تقريباً *taqriiban*
necessary ضروري *daruurii*
necessarily بالضرورة *bid-daruurah*
neck رقبة *raqaba*
necklace قلادة/سلسلة *qilaada/silsilah*
necktie ربطة عنق *rabtat `unuq*
need احتياج *ihtiyaaj*
need (v.) يحتاج/احتاج *yahtaaj/ihtaaja*
needle إبرة *ibra*
needless غني عن *ghaniy `an*
needy محتاج *muhtaaj*
negative (photo) نجتف الصور *nijaatiif as-suwar*
neighbor جار *jaar*
neighborhood حي *hay*
nephew ابن الأخ/ابن الأخت *ibn al-akh/ibn al-ukht*
never أبداً *abadan*
new جديد *jadiid*
news أخبار *akhbaar*
news stand كشك الصحف *kushik as-suhuf*
newspaper صحيفة/جريدة *sahiifa/jariida*
next اللاحق/القادم *al-laahiq/al-qaadim*
next to بجانب/بالقرب *bijaanib/bilqurb*
nice (person) طيب (جميل) *tayyib (jamiil)*
nice (pleasant) جميل (ممتع) *jamiil (mumti`)*
nicely برفق/بلطف *bilutf/birifq*
niece بنت الأخ/بنت الأخت *bint al-akh/bint al-ukht*
night ليل *layl*
night duty دوام ليلي *dawaam laylii*
nightclothes ملابس ليلية *malaabis layliyya*
nightclub نادي ليلي *naadii laylii*
nightdress لباس/فستان ليلي *libas/fustan laylii*
nightly ليلاً *laylan*
nipple (bottle) حلمة *hilma*
no لا/كلا *laa/kallaa*
no entry ممنوع الدخول *mamnuu` ad-dukhuul*
no, thank you لا شكراً *laa shukran*
no one لا أحد *laa ahad*
nobility نبل *nubl*
noise ضوضاء *dawdaa'*
non-stop (flight) دون توقف *duun tawaqquf*
noodles معكرونة *ma`karuuna*
normal طبيعي *tabii`ii*
normality حياة طبيعية *hayaat tabi`iyah*
normally عادة *`aadatan*
north شمال *shamaal*
northern شمالي *shamaaliy*
nose أنف *anf*
nose drops قطرات أنف *qatraat anf*
nosebleed نزيف أنف *naziif anf*
notebook دفتر (ملاحظات) *daftar (mulaahazaat)*

notepad مفكرة *mufak-kirah*
notepaper ورق ملاحظات *waraq mulaahazaat*
notes ملاحظات/رؤوس أقلام *mulaahazaat* **(observations)/** *ru'uus aqlaam*
notice إشعار *ish`aar*
notice (v.) يلاحظ/لاحظ *yulaahiz/laahaz*
notification إعلام *i`lam*
notify أعلم/يعلم *a`lam/yu`lim*
nothing لا شيء *laa shay'*
November تشرين الثاني/نوفمبر *nuufambar/tishriin ath-thaanii*
nowhere ليس في أي مكان *laysa fii ay-makaan*
number عدد *`adad*
number plate رقم السيارة *raqam as-sayyaara*
numbers أرقام *arqaam*
numeral رقم *raqam*
nurse ممرضة *mumarrida*
nursery حضانة *hadaanah*
nuts مكسرات *mukasaraat*
nutty جوزي *jawziy*

O
occupation وظيفة/شغل *waziifa (shughl)*
occupation (occupy a place) احتلال *ihtilaal*
occupational مهنية *mihaniya*
occupy يحتل/احتل *yahtal-lu/ihtal-la*
October تشرين الأول/أكتوبر *uktuubar/tishriin al-awwal*
off (gone bad) فاسد *faasid*
off (turned off) مغلق *mughlaq*
offer عرض *`ard*
office مكتب *maktab*
official رسمي *rasmiy*
officially رسمياً *rasmiy-yan*
oil زيت *zayt*
oil level مستوى الزيت *mustawaa az-zayt*
oily زيتي/دسم *dasim/zaytiy*
ointment مرهم *marham*
okay لا بأس/نعم *laa ba's/na`am*
old (thing) قديم *qadiim*
old (person) مسن *musin*
on, at على/عند *`alaa/`inda*
on (turned on) مفتوح/مشغل *maftuuh/mushaghal*
on board راكب *raakib*
on the left على اليسار *`alaa al-yasaar*
on the right على اليمين *`alaa al-yamiin*
on the way على الطريق *`alaat-tariiq*
oncoming car سيارة قديمة *sayyaara qaadima*
one واحد *waahid*
one-way ticket تذكرة سفر رحلة واحدة *tadhkarat safar rihla waahida*
one-way traffic حركة مرور باتجاه واحد *harakat muruur bit-tijaah waahid*
onion بصل *basal*
open مفتوح *maftuuh*
open (v.) يفتح/فتح *yaftah/fataha*
opening افتتاح *iftitaah*

operate (surgeon) يعمل عملية جراحية *ya`mal `amaliyya jiraa<u>h</u>iyya*
operation عملية *`amaliy-ah*
operator (telephone) العامل بمركز الاتصالات *al-`aamil bi-markaz al-itti<u>s</u>aalaat*
opposite عكس/مقابل *`aks/ muqaabul*
opt اختيار *i<u>kh</u>tiyaar*
optician نظاراتي *na<u>z</u>aaraatii*
option خيار *<u>kh</u>ayaar*
orange (color) برتقالي *burtuqaalii*
orange (fruit) برتقال *burtuqaal*
order أمر (طلب) *amr (<u>t</u>alab)*
order رتبة *rutba*
order (v.) يأمر/أمر *ya'mur/amara*
orderly منظم *muna<u>z</u>am*
other آخر *aa<u>kh</u>ar*
other side من جهة أخرى *min jiha u<u>kh</u>raa*
outside خارج *<u>kh</u>aarij*
over (duration) على مدى *`ala madaa*
over (finish) انتهى *intahaa*
over (above) على *`alaa*
over there هناك*hunaak*
overly مفرط *mufri<u>t</u>*
overpass معبر *ma`bar*
overseas من وراء البحار/في الخارج *min waraa'i-lbi<u>h</u>aar/fii al-<u>kh</u>aarij*
overtake يتجاوز *yatajaawaz*
oyster محار *ma<u>hh</u>aar*

P

pack حزمة *<u>h</u>uzmah*
packed lunch وجبة معلبة *wajba mu`allaba*
page صفحة *<u>s</u>af<u>h</u>a*
pain ألم *alam*
painful مؤلم/موجع *mu'lim/muuji`*
painkiller مسكن ألم *musakkin alam*
paint صبغ/دهان *dihaan/<u>s</u>ab<u>gh</u>*
painter رسام/دهان *ras-saam/ dhhaan*
painting لوحة *law<u>h</u>ah*
pajamas بيجاما *biijaama*
palace قصر *qa<u>s</u>r*
pan مقلاة *miqlaat*
pane لوح *law<u>h</u>*
panties سراويل *saraawiil*
pants بنطلون/سروال *ban<u>t</u>aluun/ sirwaal*
pantyhose جورب نسائي *jawrab nisaa'ii*
papaya بابايا *babaaya*
paper ورق *waraq*
paraffin oil زيت البرافين *zayt al-baraafiin*
parasol مظلة *mi<u>z</u>alla*
parcel *ruzma/<u>t</u>ard*
pardon عفواً *`afwan*
parenting أبوة/أمومة *ubuw-wah (father)/umumah (mother)*
parents والدان *waalidaan*
park (gardens) منتزه (حديقة) *muntazah (<u>h</u>adiiqa)*
park (v.) نوقف السيارة *nuyuqif as-sayyaara*

parking garage مرآب سيارات *mir'aab say-yaaraat*
parking space موقف سيارة *mawqif sayyaara*
part (car) جزء/قطع *qit`ah/juz'*
participation مشاركة *musharakah*
partner شريك *shariik*
party حفلة *haflah*
pass (permit) تسريح *tasriih*
passable (road) عابر *`aabir*
passenger مسافر *musaafir*
passion عاطفة *`aatifah*
passionate متحمس/متعاطف *mutaham-mis/mut`aatif*
passionfruit فاكهة العاطفة *faakihat al-`aatifah*
passport جواز سفر *jawaaz safar*
passport photo صورة جواز *suurat jawaaz*
password كلمة السر *kalimat as-sir*
patience صبر *sabr*
patient (sick) مريض *mariid*
patient (adj.) *saabir*
pay يدفع/دفع *yadfa`/dafa`a*
pay the bill دفع الفاتوة *daf` al-faatuura*
payable مستحقة الدفع *mustahaq-qted-daf`*
peach خوخ/دراق *khawkh/durraaq*
peanut فول سوداني *fuul suudaaniy*
pear إجاص *ijjaas*
pearl لؤلؤ *lu'lu'*
peas بازلاء *baazillaa'*
pedal دواسة *dawwaasa*
pedestrian crossing معبر المشاة *ma`bar al-mushah*
pedestrians مشاة *mushaat*
pedicure عناية القدم *`inaaya al-aqdaam*
pen قلم *qalam*
pencil قلم رصاص *qalam rasaas*
penknife سكين قلم *sikkiin qalam*
penis قضيب *qadiib*
people ناس *naas*
people (the) الشعب *ash-sha`b*
pepper (black) فلفل أسود *fulful aswad*
pepper (chilli) فلفل حار *fulful haar*
perform أداء *adaa'*
performance الأداء *al adaa'*
perfume عطر *`itr*
perhaps ربما/لعل *rubbamaa/la`ala*
period (menstrual) العادة الشهرية *al-`aada ash-shahriyya*
period (time) فترة *fatrah*
periodical دورية *dawriyah*
periodically دوري (بشكل) *(bishaklin) dawriy*
permission إذن *idhn*
permit رخصة/تصريح *rukhsa/tasriih*
person شخص *shakhs*
personal شخصي *shakhsii*
personally شخصياً *shakhsiyan*
personality شخصية *shakhsiy-yah*
personnel موظفين (عمال) *muwazafiin* **(civil workers/ employers)/** شؤون العمال

shu'uunal-`um-maal **(personnel or human resources)**
pet حيوان أليف *hayawaan aliif*
petrol وقود/بترول/بنزين *waquud/bitruul/banziin*
petrol station محطة نقود *mahattat waquud*
pharmacist صيدلية/صيدلي *saydaliyah* (f.)/*saydaliy*
pharmacy صيدلية *saydaliyya*
phone تليفون/هاتف *tilifun/haatif*
phone (v.) يتصل/اتصل *it-tasala/yatasil*
phone booth كشك تليفون *kishk tilifun*
phone call مكالمة هاتفية *mukalamah haatifiyyah*
phone card بطاقة شحن/بطاقة هاتفية *bitaqat shahn/bitaaqa haatifiy-yah*
phone directory دليل الأرقام *daliil al arqaam*
phone number رقم تلفون (هاتف) *raqam tilifun (haatif)*
photo صورة *suura*
photocopier آلة النسخ *aalat an-nasikh*
photocopy نسخة *nuskha*
photocopy (v.) يصور/صور *yusawwir/saw-wara*
phrase عبارة *`ibaarah*
phrasebook كتاب العبارات *kitaab al-`ibaaraat*
pick up (come to) يتسلم (يأخذ) *yatasallam (ya'khudh)*
pick up (go to) يحمل (يوصل) *yahmil (yuusil)*
picnic نزهة/رحلة *nuzhah/rihla*
pill (contraceptive) حبوب منع الحمل *hubuub man` al-hamal*
pillow مخدة *mikhadda/wisaadah*
pillowcase كيس مخدة *kiis mikhadda*
pills, tablets حبوب *hubuub*
pin دبوس *dabbuus*
pineapple أناناس *anaanaas*
pipe (plumbing) أنبوب *unbuub*
pipe (smoking) غليون *ghalyuun*
pipe tobacco تبغ غليون *tabgh al-ghalyuun*
pitiful يرثى له *yurthaa lahu*
pity شفقة *shafaqah*
place مكان *makaan*
place of interest أماكن مهمة *amaakin muhimma*
placement تنصيب *tansiib*
plain عادي *`aadiy*
plain (person, simple) صريح/ بسيط *basiit/sariih*
plain (not flavored) *biduun nakha/ta`m*
plains سهول *suhuul*
plan (intention) خطة *khut-tah*
plan (v.) خطط *khat-tata*
plan (map) مستوي *mustawii*
plane طائرة *taa'ira*
plant نبات *nabaat*
plaster cast الجبس الطبي *al-jibs at-tibbii*
plastic بلاستك *blaastik*
plastic bag كيس بلاستك *kiis*

(blaastik)
plate صحن *sahn*
platform منصة *minassa*
play (drama) مسرحية *masrahiyya*
play (v.) ألعب/لعب *al`ab/la`iba*
play golf لعب الجولف *la`ib al-gulf*
play sports يلعب/لعب رياضة *yal`ab/la`ib riyaada*
play tennis يلعب/لعب التنس *yal`ab/la`ib at-tinis*
playground منطقة لعب الأطفال/ ملعب الأطفال *mintaqat la`ib lil-atfaal/mal`ab al atfaal*
playing cards لعب الورق *la`ib al-waraq*
pleasant ممتع *mumti`*
please من فضلك *min fadlik*
pleasurable ممتع *mumti`*
pleasure متعة *mut`a*
plug (electric) القابس/واصل *al-qaabis/waasil*
plum برقوق *barquuq*
plumber سباك *sabbak*
pocket جيب *jayb*
pocketknife سكين الجيب *sikkiin al-jayb*
pockets جيوب *juyuub*
point out أشار *ashaarar*
poison سم *sum*
poisonous سام *saam*
police شرطة *shurta*
police car سيارة الشرطة *siyayaratush-shurtah*
police officer ضابط شرطة *daabit shurta*
police station مركز الشرطة *markaz ash-shurta*
policeman شرطي *shurtiy*
pond بركة *birka*
ponder فكر/يفكر *fak-kara/yufak-kir*
pony حصان صغير/مهر *muhr/hisaan saghiir*
popular شعبي *sha`biy*
popularity شعبية *sha`biy-yah*
population الكثافة السكانية *al-kathaafa as-sukkaaniyyah*
porcupine النيص/شيهم *shayham/an-niis*
porcine خنزيري *khinziiriy*
pork لحم خنزير *lahm khinziir*
port ميناء *miinaa'*
porter (concierge) بواب *baw-waab*
porter (for bags) حمال *hammaal*
possibility إمكانية *imkaaniy-yah*
possible ممكن *mumkin*
post (v.) أرسل/يرسل بالبريد *arsal/yursil bilbariid*
post office مكتب البريد *maktab bariid*
postage أجرة البريد/طوابع بريدية *ujrat' al-bariid/tawabi` baridiy-yah*
postbox صندوق بريد *sunduuq bariid*
postcard بطاقة بريدية *bitaaqa bariidiyya*
postcode رمز بريدي *ramz bariidii*

postpone يؤجل *yu'ajjil*
potato بطاطس *bataatis*
potato chips بطاطس مقلية *bataatis maqliya*
poultry دواجن *dawaajin*
powder مسحوق *mashoouq*
powdered milk حليب مجفف *haliib mujaffaf*
power طاقة *taaqah*
power (control) سلطة *sultah*
power outlet مخرج الكهرباء *makhraj al-kahrabaa'*
prawn جمبري *jambarii*
precious ثمين *thamiin*
precious metal معدن ثمين *ma`dan thamiin*
precious stone حجر ثمين *hajar thamiin*
prefer فضّل/يفضّل *fad-dal/yufaddil*
preferable من الأفضل *minal'afdal*
preference الأفضلية *al-afdaliy-yah*
pregnancy حمل *haml*
pregnant حامل *haamil*
prescribe يصف/يكتب وصفة *yasif/yaktub wasfah*
prescription وصفة *wasfah*
present (v.) تقديم/عرض *taqdiim/`ard*
present (gift) هدية *hadiyya*
present (here) موجود *mawjuud*
present (tense) الحاضر *al haadir*
presentation عرض/تقديم *`ard/taqdiim*
presenter مقدم *muqa-ddim*
press (v.) تلفظ *yadghat*
pressure ضغط *daght*
prestige هيبة *haybah*
prestigious مرموق *marmuqa*
price ثمن/سعر *thaman/si`r*
price list قائمة أسعار *qaa'imat as`aar*
priceless لا تقدر بثمن *laa tuqad-dar bithaman*
prices أسعار *as`aar*
print (picture) يطبع/طبع *yatba`/taba`a*
print (v.) يطبع *yatba`*
printer طابعة *tabi`a*
probability احتمال *ihtimaal*
probably محتمل *muhtamal*
problem مشكلة *mushkila*
problems مشاكل/مشكلات *mashaakil/mushkilat*
profession مهنة (حرفة) *mihna (hirfa)*
professional كفأ *kuf'*
professionalism كفاءة مهنية *kfaa'ah mihaniy-yah*
profit فائدة *faa'ida*
program برنامج *barnaamaj*
pronounce يتلفظ *talaf-faza*
pronunciation نطق *nutq*
propane غاز البروبين *ghaaz al-brubiin*
pudding كعك/حلوى *ka`ik/halwaa*
pull يسحب *yas-hab*
pull a muscle تمطط العضلة *tamattut al-'adalah*

pulsation نبض *nabd*
pulse نبض *nabd*
pure نقي *naqii*
purification تنقية *tanqiy-yah*
purify ينقي *yunaq-qii*
purple بنفسجي *banafsajii*
purse (for money) محفظة *mihfazah*
purse (handbag) حقيبة *haqiiba*
push يدفع/دفع *yadfa`/dafa`*
puzzle لغز *lughz*
puzzles ألغاز *alghaaz*
pyramid هرم *haram*
pyramids أهرام/أهرامات *ahraamaat/ahraam*
pyjamas بيجامة *biijaamah*

Q
quail (bird) السمان *as-samaan*
quail (retreat) يتراجع *yataraaja`*
quarter ربع *rub`*
quarter of an hour ربع ساعة *rub` saa`a*
queen ملكة *malika*
question (v.) سأل/يسأل *sa'la/ ys`al*
question سؤال *su'aal*
quick سريع *sari`*
quickly بسرعة *bisur`ah*
quiet هادي/ساكت *haadi'/saakit*
quietly بهدوء *bihuduu'*
quill ريشة *riishah*
quilt لحاف/غطاء *ghitaa'/ lihaaf*

R
radio مذياع (راديو) *midhyaa` (radyu)*
radiologist طبيب أشعة *tabiib ashi`ah*
radiology قسم الأشعة *qism al-ashi`ah*
railroad, railway سكة القطار / سكة الحديد *sikkat al-qitaar/sikatu al hadiid*
rain مطر *matar*
rain (v.) تمطر *tumtir/mat-tara*
raincoat معطف مطري *mi`taf matariy*
rainy ممطر *mumtir*
rape اغتصاب *ightisaab*
rapid سريع *sari`*
rapidly بسرعة *bisur`ah*
rash (adj.) متهور *mutahaw-wir*
rash (n.) التهاب جلدي *iltihaab jildiy*
rat جرد *juradh*
raw خام *khaam*
razor مكنة حلاقة *makiintu hilaaqah*
razor blade شفرة حلاقة *shafrat hilaaqa*
read يقرأ/قرأ *yaqra'/qara'a*
ready جاهز/جاهزة *jaahiz/jaahiza* (f.)
reality حقيقة *haqiiqah*
really حقاً *haq-qan*
reason سبب *sabab*
receipt وصل *wasl*
reception desk الاستعلامات *al-isti`laamaat*

recipe وصفة *wasfa*

recline اتكأ/يتكئ *it-taka'a/yat-taki'*

reclining chair كرسي مستلقي *kursii mustalqi*

recommend ينصح/نصح *yansah/nasaha*

recommendation توصية *tawsiy-yah*

rectangle مستطيل *mustatiil*

red eye عين حمراء *`ayn hamraa'*

red (f.) حمراء *hamraa'*

reduce تقليل/تخفيض *taqliil/takhfiid*

reduction انخفاض/تخفيض *inkhifaad/takhfiid*

refrigerate تبريد/تثليج *tabriid/tathliij*

refrigerator ثلاجة *thallaaja*

refund إعادة/رد مال *i`aadat/rad maal*

regards تحيات *tahiyyat*

region منطقة *mantiqa*

regional إقليمي/إقليمية *iqlimiy/iqlimiy-yah* (f.)

register سجل/يسجل *saj-jala/yusaj-jil*

registered مسجل *musajjal*

registration تسجيل *tasjiil*

relative نسبي *nisbiy*

relative (member) قريب *qariib*

relatively نسبياً *nisbiy-yan*

reliable موثوق *mawthuuq*

religion دين *diin*

religiously بأمانة/بضمير *bi-amaanah/bi-dmiir*

rely اعتمد/يعتمد *i`tamad/ya`tamid*

rent إيجار *iijaar*

rent out يستأجر/استأجر *yasta'jir/ista'jar*

repair يصلح/أصلح *yuslih/aslaha*

repairs ترميم/إصلاحات *tarmiim/islaahaat*

repeat يعيد/أعاد *yu`iid/a`aada*

repetition إعادة *i`aadah*

report (v.) بلغ *bal-lagha*

report بلاغ *balaagh*

report (office) تقرير *taqriir*

report (police) محضر *mahdar*

reservation (hotel) حجز *hajz*

reservations (doubt) تحفظات *tahafuzaat*

reserve يحجز/حجز *yahjiz/hajaza*

responsibility مسؤولية *mas'uuliy-yah*

responsible مسؤول *mas'uul*

rest إستراحة *istiraaha*

rest (v.) استراح/يستريح *istaraaha/yastarih*

restaurant مطعم *mat`am*

restful مريح *muriih*

restless قلق *qaliq*

restroom مرافق صحية *maraafiq sihhiyya*

result نتيجة *natiija*

results نتائج *nataa'ij*

retired متقاعد *mutaqaa`id*

retirement تقاعد *taqaa`ud*

return رجوع/عودة *ruju`/`awdah*

return ticket تذكرة ذهاب و إياب *tadhkarah dhahaab wa iyaab*

reverse (car) يرجع إلى الوراء *yurji` 'ilaa al-waraa'*
reverse عكس *`aks*
rheumatism ألم المفاصل *alam al-mafaasil*
ribbon شريط *shariit*
rice (cooked) أرز *aruz*
rice (grain) حبوب الأرز *hubuub al-aruz*
ridicule سخرية *sukhriya*
ridicule (v.) سخر من *sakhira min*
ridiculous سخيف *sakhiif*
ride (v.) ركب/يركب *rakiba/yarkab*
ride ركوب *rukub*
riding (horseback) راكب *raakib*
right (correct) صحيح *sahiih*
right (side) يمين *yamiin*
right away فوراً *fawran*
right of way أولوية العبور *awlawiyyat al-`ubuur*
rightfully حقاً *haqan*
rinse يشطف *yashtif*
ripe ناضج *naadij*
risk خطر *khatar*
risky خطير *khatiir*
river نهر *nahr*
road طريق *tariiq*
roadway طريق *tariiq*
roast شوي/تحمير *shawy/tahmiir*
roasted محمص *muhammas*
rock (stone) صخرة *sakhra*
rocky صخري *sakhriy*
roll (bread) رغيف *raghiif*
roll (v.) لف/يلف *laf-fa/yalif-fu*
roll لفة *laf-fah*
roof سقف *saqf*
roof rack سقف السيارة *saqf as-sayyaara*
room غرفة *ghurfa*
room number رقم الغرفة *raqam al-ghurfa*
room service خدمة الغرفة *khidmat al-ghurfa*
roomy واسع/فسيح *waasi`/fasiih*
rope حبل *habl*
route طريق *tariiq*
row جدف/يجدف *jad-dafa/yujad-dif*
rowing boat زورق تجديف *zawraq tajdiif*
rubber مطاط *mattat*
rude وقح/غير مهذب *waqih/ghayr muhadhab*
ruin (v.) خرب/يخرب *khar-raba/yukhar-rib*
ruins أطلال/آثار *atlaal/aathaar*
run (v.) ركض/يركض *rakada/yarkud*
running shoes حذاء ركض *hidhaa' rakd*

S

sad حزين *haziin*
sadness حزن *huzn*
sadly للأسف *lil'asaf*
safe آمن *aamin*
safe (for cash) خزانة حديدية *khizaana hadiidiya*
safely بأمان *bi'amaan*
safety سلامة/بأمان *salaama/bi'amaan*

safety pin دبوس الأمان *dabbous al-amaan*
sail (v.) سفر بحري *safar bahriy*
sail شراع *shiraa`*
sailing boat مركب شراعي *markab shira`iy*
sailor بحار *bah-har*
salad سلطة *salata*
sale بيع *bay`*
sales مبيعات *mabii`aat*
sales (clearance) تخفيضات *takhfidaat*
sales clerk البائع *al-baa'i`*
salt ملح *milh*
salty مالح *maalih*
same نفس/مشابه *mushaabih/nafs*
sand رمال *rimaal*
sandals صندل (خف) *sandal (khuf)*
sandy beach ساحل رملي *saahil ramlii*
sanitary صحي *sih-hiy*
sanitary towel المنديل الصحي *al-mindiil as-sih-hiy*
satisfy (a request) تلبية الطلب *talabiyatu at-talab*
satisfy (v.) أرضى/يرضي *ardaa/yurdii*
Saturday (يوم) السبت *(Yawmu) As-sabt*
sauce مرق *maraq*
sauce صلصة *salsa*
sauna حمام بخاري *hammaam bukhaarii*
say يقول/قال *yaquul/qaal*
scald (injury) حرق *harq*
scales ميزان *miizaan*
scandal فضيحة *fadiihah*
scanner ماسح ضوئي *maasih daw`ii*
scarf (headscarf) حجاب *hijab*
scarf (muffler) قناع *qinaa`*
scene منظر *manzar*
scenic view منظر خلاب *manzar khallaab*
scenic walk طريق خلاب *tariiq khallaab*
scholar باحث/عالم *baahith/`aalim*
scholarship منحة (دراسية) *minha (diraasiy-yah)*
scholarship علم *`ilm*
school مدرسة *madrasa*
scissors مقص *miqas*
Scotland اسكتلندا *Iskutlandaa*
Scottish اسكتلندي *Iskutlandiy*
Scottish اسكتلندية *Iskutlandiy-yah*
screw برغي *burghii*
screwdriver مفتاح براغي *miftah baraaghii*
scuba diving الغوص *al-ghaws*
sculpture نحت *naht*
sea بحر *bahr*
search بحث *bahth*
seasick مرض الإبحار *marad al-ibhaar*
seat مقعد *maq`ad*
second (in line) ثاني *thaanii*
second (instant) ثانية *thaaniya*
secondly ثانياً *thaaniyan*
second-hand مستعمل *musta`mal*
seconds ثواني *thawaanii*

sedation تخدير *ta<u>kh</u>dhiir*
sedative مسكن/مسكنات *musakkin/musak-kinaat*
see رأى/يرى *ra'aa/yaraa*
send رسل *arasala*
sentence حكم *<u>h</u>ukm*
sentence (writing) جملة *jumla*
sentences أحكام *a<u>h</u>kaam*
sentences جمل *jumal*
separate يفصل/منفصل *yaf<u>s</u>il/munfa<u>s</u>il*
September آب/سبتمبر *Aab/Sebtamber*
serious خطير *<u>kh</u>a<u>t</u>iir*
seriously بجد/بجدية *bijad-diyah/bijad-din*
service خدمة *<u>kh</u>idma*
service station محطة بنزين *ma<u>h</u>a<u>tt</u>at banziin*
services خدمات *<u>kh</u>adamaat*
serviette منديل المائدة *mindiil al-maa'ida*
sesame oil زيت السمسم *zayt as-simsim*
sesame seeds سمسم *simsim*
set مجموعة/رزمة *majmuu`ah/ruzma*
sew يخيط/خاط *ya<u>kh</u>ii<u>t</u>/<u>kh</u>aa<u>t</u>*
sewing machine مكنة خياطة *makinat <u>kh</u>ayaa<u>t</u>ah*
shade ظل *<u>z</u>il*
shallow ضحل *<u>d</u>a<u>h</u>l*
shame عار *`aar*
shameful معيب *mu`iib*
shampoo شامبو/غسول *<u>sh</u>ambu/<u>gh</u>asuul*
shark (سمك) القرش *(samak) al qirsh*
shave يحلق الذقن *ya<u>h</u>liq a<u>dh</u>-<u>dh</u>aqn*
shaver آلة حلاقة *'aalat <u>h</u>ilaaqah*
shaving cream صابون حلاقة *<u>s</u>aabuun <u>h</u>ilaaqah*
sheet شرشف/لحاف *<u>sh</u>ar<u>sh</u>af/li<u>h</u>aaf*
sheet (paper) ورقة *waraqa*
shirt قميص *qamii<u>s</u>*
shoe polish صبغ/دهن حذاء *sib<u>gh</u>/dihn <u>h</u>i<u>dh</u>aa'*
shoes أحذية *a<u>dh</u>iyah*
shop, store مخزن/متجر *ma<u>kh</u>zan/matjar*
shop (v.) يتسوق *yatasawwaq*
shop assistant بائع *baa'i`*
shopping center مركز تسوق *markaz tasawwuq (as-suuq)*
shop window نافذة الدكان *naafi<u>dh</u>at ad-dukkan*
short قصير *qa<u>s</u>iir*
short circuit دائرة كهربائية *daa'ira kahrbaa'iyya*
shorts (short trousers) شورت *shoort*
shorts (underpants) سروال تحتي/داخلي قصير *sirwaal ta<u>h</u>tii/daa<u>kh</u>iliy qa<u>s</u>iir*
shoulder كتف *katif*
shoulders كتفان *katifaan*
show (v.) أظهر *a<u>z</u>hara*
show عرض *`ar<u>d</u>*
shower دش *du<u>sh</u>*
shrimp روبيان/جمبري *ruubyaan/jambari*

shutter (camera/on window) مصراع *mi_s_raa`*
sieve منخل *mun_kh_ul*
sightseeing التنزه *at-tanazzuh*
sign علامة *`alaama*
sign (light) إشارة *i_sh_aarah*
sign (v.) يوقع/وقع *yuwaqqi`/waq-qa`a*
signature توقيع/أمضى *tawqii`/im_dh_aa'*
silence صمت *_s_amt*
silk حرير *_h_ariir*
silver فضة *fi_dd_a*
simple بسيط *basii_t_*
simplify تبسيط *tabsii_t_*
single (only one) واحد *waa_h_id*
single (f.) واحدة *waa_h_idah*
single (unmarried) أعزب *a`zab*
single (unmarried) عزباء *`azbaa'*
single ticket تذكرة واحدة *ta_dh_kara waa_h_ida*
sir سيد *sayyid*
sister أخت *u_kh_t*
sister حاضنة *haa_d_inah*
sisterhood أخوّة *u_kh_uw-wah*
sit (v.) جلس *jalasa*
sit down اجلس *ijlis*
sitter أخوات *a_kh_awaat*
size حجم *_h_ajm*
skiing تزلج *tazalluj*
skin جلد *jild*
skinny نحيف/نحيفة *na_h_iif/na_h_iifah* (f.)
skirt تنورة *tannuura*
sleep ينام/نام *yanaam/naama*
sleeping car عربة نوم *`arabat nawm*
sleeping pills حبوب منومة *_h_ubuub munawwima*
sleepy نعسان *na`saan*
sleeve كم *kum*
slip ينزلق *yanzaliq*
slippers خف *_kh_uf*
slow بطيء *ba_t_ii'*
slow train قطار بطيء *qi_t_aar ba_t_ii'*
small صغير *_s_a_gh_iir*
small change عملة صغيرة *`umla _s_a_gh_iira*
smartphone هاتف ذكي *hatif _dh_akii*
smell رائحة *raa'i_h_a*
smell (v.) شم/يشم *_sh_am-ma/ya_sh_ummu*
smelly رائحة كريهة *rai'_h_ah karihah*
smoke دخان *du_kh_-_kh_aan*
smoke (cigarettes) تدخين *tad_kh_iin*
smoke detector منبه دخان *munabbih du_kh_aan*
smoker مدخن *muda_kh_-_kh_in*
snake حية/ثعبان *_h_ayya/_th_u`baan*
snorkel أنبوب تنفس/سنوركل *unbuub tanaffus/snurkul*
snorkeling غطس بأنبوب التنفس *_gh_a_t_s (bi unbuub at-tanafus)*
snow ثلج *_th_alj*
snow (v.) تثلج *tu_th_lij*
soap صابون *_s_aabuun*
soap powder مسحوق صابون *ma_sh_uuq _s_aabuun*
soccer كرة القدم *kurat al-qadam*

soccer match مباراة كرة قدم *mubaaraat kurat qadam*
social networks شبكة التواصل الاجتماعي *shabakaat al-tawasul al-ijtimaa`ii*
socket (electric) مقبس *miqbas*
socks جوارب *jawaarib*
soft لين *lay-yin*
soft drink مشروب غازي *mashruub ghaaziy*
sole (of shoe) نعل *na`l*
some بعض *ba`d*
someone شخص ما *shakhs maa*
sometimes أحياناً *ahyaanan*
somewhere في مكان ما *fii makaanin maa*
son ابن *ibn*
soon عن قريب *`an qariib*
sore (painful) ألم *alam*
sore (ulcer) التهاب *iltihaab*
sore throat التهاب الحنجرة *iltihaab al-hunjurah*
sorrow حزن *huzn*
sorry آسف *aasif*
soup شوربة (حساء) *shuurba (hisaa')*
sour حامض *haamid*
south جنوب *januub*
souvenir تذكار *tidhkaar*
soy الصويا *as-suyaa*
soy bean فول الصويا *fuul as-suyaa*
span امتداد/امتد *imtidaad/imtad-da*
spanner, wrench مفتاح ربط *miftaah rabt*
spare احتياطي/إضافي *ihtiyaatii/idaafii*
spare parts قطع غيار *qita` ghiyaar*
spare time وقت فراغ *waqt faraagh*
spare tire إطار احتياطي *itaar ihtiyaatii*
spare wheel عجلة احتياطية *`ajala ihtiyaatiyya*
speak يتكلم/تكلم/تحدث *yatkallam/takallam/tahad-dath*
special خاص *khaas*
specialist متخصص *mutakhas-sis*
specialist (doctor) أخصائي *akhissaa'ii*
speciality تخصص *takhas-sus*
speciality (cooking) طبخ خاص *tabkh khaas*
speed سرعة *sur`ah*
speed limit حد السرعة *hadd as-sur`a*
spell يتلفظ/تلفظ *yatalaffaz/talaf-faz*
spelling إملاء *imlaa'*
sphinx أبو الهول *abu al-haul*
spices توابل *tawaabil*
spicy حار *haar*
splinter شظية *shaziy-yah*
spoon ملعقة *mil`aqa*
sport رياضة *riyaada*
sports center مركز رياضة *markaz riyaadah*
spot (place) موقع *mawqi`*
spot (stain) بقعة *buq`ah*
spouse زوج/قرين *zawj/qariin*
sprain التواء *iltiwaa'*
spring (device) نابض *naabid*

spring (season) (فصل) الربيع *(faslu) ar- rabii`*
square (plaza) ساحة *saa<u>h</u>a*
square (shape) مربع *murabba`*
square meter متر مربع *mitr murabba`*
squash (game) الإسكواش *al-iskwaa<u>sh</u>*
squash (vegetable) يقطين/كوسا *yaq<u>t</u>iin/kuusah*
stadium ملعب *mal`ab*
stain بقعة *buq`ah*
stain remover مزيل البقع *muziil al-buqa`*
stairs سلم/درج *sullam/daraj*
stamp طابع *<u>t</u>aabi`*
stand (be standing) وقف/يقف *waqafa/yaqif*
stand up قم/يقوم/قام *qum/yaquum/qaama*
star نجمة *najmah*
starfruit الغلال النجمية *al-<u>gh</u>ilaal an-najmiyya*
stars نجوم *nujuum*
start بدأ/يبدأ *bada'/yabda'*
start (a) بداية *bidaayah*
station محطة *ma<u>h</u>a<u>t</u>tah*
statue تمثال *tim<u>th</u>aal*
stay (in hotel) يقيم/أقام *yuqiim/aqaama*
stay (remain) يبقى/بقي *yabqaa/baqiya*
steal يسرق *yasriq*
steam بخار *bu<u>kh</u>aar*
steel فولاذ *fuulaa<u>dh</u>*
step خطوة *<u>kh</u>u<u>t</u>wa*
step (v.) خطى/يخطو *<u>kh</u>a<u>t</u>aa/ya<u>kh</u><u>t</u>uu*
stepfather زوج الأم *zawj al-um*
stepmother زوجة الأب *zawjat al-ab*
steps خطوات/درجات *darajaat/<u>kh</u>u<u>t</u>uwaat*
sterilize يعقم/عقم *yu`aqqim/`aq-qama*
stick عصى *`a<u>s</u>aa*
stick (attach) يلصق *yul<u>s</u>iq*
sticking plaster ضماد لاصق *<u>d</u>amaad laa<u>s</u>iq*
sticky tape شريط لاصق *<u>sh</u>arii<u>t</u> laa<u>s</u>iq*
stir-fried مقلي *maqlii*
stitch غرز *<u>gh</u>urzah*
stitches (wound) غرزة *<u>gh</u>uraz*
stomach (abdomen) بطن *ba<u>t</u>n*
stomach (organ) معدة *ma`ida*
stomach ache ألم المعدة *alam al-ma`ida*
stomach cramps مغص *ma<u>ghs</u>*
stool مقعد *maq`ad*
stools براز *buraaz*
stop (bus-) موقف (محطة) *mawqif (ma<u>h</u>a<u>t</u>ta)*
stop (cease) يتوقف/توقف *yatawaqqaf/tawaqqafa*
stop (halt) يوقف *yuuqif*
stopover متوقف *mutawaqqif*
storage تخزين *ta<u>kh</u>ziin*
store, shop مخزن/محل *ma<u>kh</u>zan/ma<u>h</u>all*
storey طابق *<u>t</u>aabiq*
stories (levels) طوابق *<u>t</u>awaabiq*

stories (literature) قصص *qisas*
storm عاصفة *`aasifa*
story قصة *qis-sah*
straight مستقيم *mustaqiim*
straight ahead مباشرة *mubaasharatan*
straw (drinking) مصاصة شرب *massaasat shurb*
straw قش *qash*
street شارع *shaari`*
street vendor بائع متجول *baa'i` mutajawwil*
streets شوارع *shawaari`*
strength قوة *quw-wah*
strike (work stoppage) إضراب *idraab*
string خيط/حبل *khayt/habl*
strong قوي *qawii*
study دراسة *diraasa*
study درس/يدرس *darasa/yadrus*
studies دراسات *diraasaat*
stuffed محشو/محشوة *mahshuw/ mahshuwah* (f.)
stuffed animal حيوان محشو *hayawaan mahshuu*
stuffing الحشو *al-hashuu*
subtitles ترجمة الأفلام *tarjamat al-aflaam*
subway قطار الأنفاق/الميترو *qitar al anfaaq/ al miitruu*
succeed ينجح/نجح *yanjah/ najaha*
successful ناجح *naajih*
sugar سكر *sukkar*
suit بدلة *badla*
suitcase حقيبة *haqiiba*
suite جناح *janaah*
summer (فصل) الصيف *(fasl) as-sayf*
sun شمس *shams*
sunbathe حمام شمسي *ham-maam shamsiy*
Sunday (يوم) الأحد *(yawm) al-ahad*
sunglasses نظارات شمسية *nazzaaraat shamsiyya*
sunhat قبعة شمسية *qubba`a shamsiyya*
sunny مشمس *mushmis*
sunrise شروق الشمس *shuruuq ashshams*
sunscreen مرهم ضد الشمس *marham did ash-shams*
sunset غروب *ghuruub*
sunshade (protection from the sun وقى من الشمس *waqaa` min ash-shams***)**
sunshade (umbrella) مظلة *mizallah*
sunstroke ضربة شمس *darbat shams*
suntan اسمرار البشرة *ismiraar al bashara*
suntan lotion مستحضر اسمرار البشرة *mustahdar ismiraar al-bashara*
suntan oil زيت اسمرار البشرة *zayt ismiraar al basharah*
supermarket السوق المركزية *as-suuq al-markaziyya*
surcharge أجرة إضافية *ujra idaafiyya*

surf (big waves) رياضة ركوب الأمواج *riyaadat rukuub al amwaajj*
surf (the web) تصفح *tasaf-fuh*
surface mail البريد العادي *al-bariid al-`aadi*
surfboard لوح التزلج على الأمواج *lawh at-tazalluj `alaa al-amuwaaj*
surname اللقب *al-laqab*
surprise, a مفاجأة *mufaaja'a*
surprise (v.) فاجأ/يفاجئ *faaja'/yufaaji'*
surprises مفاجآت *mufaja'aat*
swallow يبلع *yabla`*
swamp مستنقع *mustanqa`*
swap (change) تغيير *taghyiir*
sweat عرق *`araq*
sweat (v.) يعرق/عرق *ya`raq/`ariqa*
sweater سترة (بلوز) *sitrah (bluuz)*
sweet حلو *huluw*
sweetcorn ذرة حلوة *dhura hulwa*
sweets حلويات *halawiyyaat*
swim يسبح *yasbah/sabaha*
swimmer سباح *sab-bah*
swimming costume زي سباحة *zay sibaaha*
swimming pool حوض سباحة/ مسبح *hawd sibaaha/masbah*
swindle خدعة *khud`ah*
swindle (v.) خدع/يخدع *khada`a/yakhda`u*
switch مفتاح *miftaah*
switch (v.) تغيير/تبديل *taghyiir/tabdiil*
synagogue معبد يهودي *ma`bad yahuudii*
syrup شراب *sharaab*
syrup (medicine) شراب دواء *sharaab dawaa'*

T

table منضدة/طاولة/مائدة *mindada/taawilah/maa'idah*
table tennis كرة الطاولة *kurat at-taawila*
tablecloth مفرش *mafrash*
tablemat غطاء المنضدة/المائدة *ghitaa' al-mindada/almaa'idah*
tablespoon ملعقة طعام *mil`aqa ta`aam*
tablet (computer) حاسوب لوحي *haasuub lawhii*
tablets حبوب/أقراص *hubuub/aqraas*
take (medicine) يأخذ/أخذ *ya'khudh/akhadha*
take (photo) يلتقط صورة *yaltaqit*
take (time) يستغرق *yastaghriq*
talk تحدث/يتحدث *tahaddatha/yatahaddath*
talkative ثرثار *tharthaar*
tall طويل *tawiil*
tampon سدادة *saddaada*
tanned (leather) مدبوغ *madbuugh*
tanned (skin) مسمر *musmarr*
tap حنفية *hanafiyya*
tap water ماء حنفية *maa' al-hanafiyya*
tape شريط لاصق *shariit lasiq*
tape measure شريط قياس *shariit qiyaas*
taste طعم/ذوق *ta`am/dhwaq*

taste (v.) يذوق *yadhuuq*
tax ضريبة *dariiba*
taxes ضرائب *daraa'ib*
tax-free shop دكان بدون ضريبة *dukkaan biduun dariiba*
taxi تاكسي (سيارة أجرة) *taksi (sayyaarat ujra)*
taxi stand موقف تاكسي *mawqif taksii*
tea (black) شاي *shaay*
tea (green) شاي أخضر *shaay akhdar*
teacup كوب شاي *kuub shaay*
teapot إبريق شاي *ibriiq shaay*
teaspoon ملعقة شاي *mil`aqat shaay*
teat (bottle) حلمة *hilma*
telephoto lens عدسة جهاز الفوتوغراف *`adasat jihaaz al-futughraaf*
television تلفزيون/تلفاز *tilifizyuun/tilfaaz*
temperature (body) درجة حرارة (الجسم) *darajat haraarat (al jism)*
temperature (heat) درجة حرارة (الجو) *darajat haraarat (al jaw)*
temple معبد *ma`bad*
temporarily مؤقتاً *mu'aqqatan*
temporary filling حشوة مؤقتة *hashwa mu'aqqata*
temptation إغراء *ighraa'*
ten عشرة *`asharah*
tender, sore ألم *alam*
tender (adj.) طيب/طيبة *tay-yib/tayyibah* (f.)
tender, give (v.) أعطى/سلم *a`taa/sal-lama*
tennis تنس *tinnis*
tent خيمة *khayma*
terminus نهاية خط الرحلة *nihaayat khat ar-rihla*
terrace شرفة *shurfah*
terrible رهيب/فظيع *rahiib/fazii`*
terribly (بشكل) رهيب *(bishakl) rahiib*
thank (v.) شكر/يشكر *shakar/yashkur*
thank you شكراً *shukran*
thaw ذوبان *dhawabaan*
theater مسرح *masrah*
theft سرقة *sariqa*
there هناك *hunaaka*
thermometer (body) ميزان الحرارة *miizaan al-haraara*
thermometer (weather) الترمومتر *at-tirmumitr*
thick سميك *samiik*
thief لص *lis*
thigh فخذ *fakhidh*
thin (not fat) نحيف/نحيفة *nahiif/nahiifah* (f.)
thin (not thick) رقيق/رقيقة *raqiiq/raqiiqah* (f.)
think (believe) يظن *yazun*
think (ponder) فكر/يفكر *fakkar/yufakkir*
third (1/3) ثلث *thuluth*
thirsty عطشان *`atshaan*
this هذه/هذا *haadhaa/haadhihi (f)*
this afternoon بعد ظهر اليوم *ba`da zuhr al-yawm*

this evening هذا المساء *haadhaa al-masaa'*
this morning هذا الصباح *haadhaa as-sabaah*
thread خيط *khayt*
throat حنجرة *hunjura*
thunder رعد *ra`d*
thunderstorm عاصفة رعدية *`aasifa ra`diyya*
Thursday (يوم) الخميس *(yawm) al-khamiis*
ticket بطاقة/تذكرة الدخول/ تذكرة سفر *bitaaqa/tadhkarat ad-dukhuul/tadhkarat safar*
ticket (admission) تذكرة الدخول *tadhkarat safar*
ticket (travel) تذكرة سفر *tadhkarat safar*
ticket (traffic) غرامة *gharaamah*
ticket office مكتب تذاكر *maktab tadhaakir*
tides المد و الجزر *al madd wa ljazr*
tidy منظم/مرتب *murat-tab/ munaz-zam*
tie (necktie) رباط العنق *ribaat al-`unuq*
tie (v.) يشد/يربط *yashudd (yarbut)*
tights جوارب *jawaarib*
time وقت *waqt*
time (occasion) مناسبة *munaasaba*
times (multiplying) ضرب (في) *darb (fii)*
timetable جدول الضرب *jadwal ad-darb*
tin (can) علبة *`ulba*
tip (gratuity) إكرامية/بقشيش *ikraamiyya/baqshiish*
tire إطار *itaar*
tire pressure مستوى الهواء بالإطار *mustawaa al-hawaa' bil-itaar*
tissues محارم *mahaarim*
tobacco تبغ *tabgh*
today اليوم *al-yawm*
toddler طفل صغير *tifl saghiir*
toe إصبع القدم *isba` al-qadam*
to (direction) إلى *'ilaa*
together مع بعض *maa` ba`d*
toilet المرحاض/التواليت *al-mirhaad/at-tuwaaliit*
toilet paper ورق تواليت *waraq tuwaaliit*
toilet seat كرسي التواليت *kursii at-tuwaaliit*
toiletries مساحيق *masaahiiq*
tomato طماطم *tamaatim*
tomorrow غداً *ghadan*
tongue لسان *lisaan*
tonight هذه الليلة *haadhihi al-layla*
tool أداة *adaat*
tooth/teeth سن/أسنان *sin/asnaan*
toothache ألم أسنان *alam asnaan*
toothbrush فرشاة أسنان *furshaat asnaan*
toothpaste معجون أسنان *ma`juun asnaan*
toothpick عود تنظيف الأسنان *`uud tanziif al-asnaan*
top قمة *qimma*
torch, flashlight مشعل، مصباح يدوي *mish`al, misbaah yadawii*

total مجموع *majmuu`*
tough خشن *khashin*
tough (hard) صعب *sa`b*
tour رحلة سياحية *rihla siyaahiyya*
tour guide دليل سياحة *daliil siyaaha*
tourist سائح *saa'ih*
tourist class درجة سياحية *daraja siyaahiy-yah*
tourist information office مكتب معلومات السياح *maktab ma`luumaat as-suyyaah*
tow يسحب (يجر) *yas-hab (yajur)*
tow cable سلك سحب *silk sahb*
towel منشفة *minshafa*
tower برج *burj*
town بلدة (مدينة) *balda (madiina)*
town hall قاعة البلدية *qa`aat al-baladiyya*
toy لعبة *lu`ba*
traffic حركة المرور *harakat al-muruur*
traffic light إشارة ضوئية/مرور *ishaara daw'iyya/muruur*
train قطار *qitaar*
train station محطة القطار *mahattat al-qitaar*
train ticket تذكرة القطار *tadhkarat al qitaar*
train timetable جدول القطار *jadwal al-qitaar*
translate ترجم/يترجم *tarjama/ yutarjim*
translation ترجمة *tarjamah*
travel سفر *safar*
travel (v.) سافر/يسافر *saafara/ yusaafir*
travel agency مكتب سياحي *maktab siy-yaahiy*
travel agent وكيل سياحي *wakiil siyaahiy*
traveler مسافر *musaafir*
traveler's cheque شيك سياحي *shiik siyaahii*
travelers مسافرين/مسافرون *musaafiriin/musaafiruun*
treat عامل/يعامل *`aamala/ yu`aamil*
treatment معاملة *mu`aamala*
trial محاكمة *muhaakamah*
triangle مثلث *muthallath*
trim (haircut) شذب الشعر *shathb (ash-sha`r)*
trip رحلة *rihla*
truck شاحنة *shaahina*
trust يثق/ثقة *yathiqu* **(to trust)**/ *thiqah*
trust (n.) ثقة *thiqah*
trust (v.) وثق *wathaqa*
trustworthy موثوق فيه *mawthuuq fiih*
try on قس/قاس/يقيس *qis/qaasa/ yaqiis*
tube أنبوب *unbuub*
tube (glue) أنبوب (صمغ) *unbuub (samagh)*
Tuesday يوم (الثلاثاء) *(yawm) Ath-thulaathaa'*
tuna سمك التونا *samak at-tunah*

tunnel نفق *nafaq*
turn دار/يدير *daara/yudiru*
turn (off) أطفأ (أغلق) *(aghlaqa) atfa'a*
turn on فتح *fataha*
turn over قلب *qalaba*
TV تلفزيون/تلفاز *tilifizyuun/tilfaaz*
TV guide دليل تلفزيون/تلفاز *daliil tilifizyuun/tilfaaz*
tweet تغريدة *taghriidah*
tweet (v.) غرد *ghar-rada*
tweezers ملقط صغير *milqat saghiir*
twin(s) توأم *taw'am*
twin-bedded فراش/سرير مزدوج *firaash/sariir muzdawaj*
Twitter تويتر *Twitter*
typhoon إعصار *i`saar*

U
ugly قبيح *qabiih*
ulcer قرحة *qarhah*
umbrella مظلة *mizalla*
under تحت *tahta*
underpants ملابس داخلية *malaabis daakhiliyya*
underpass نفق *nafaq*
understand يفهم/فهم *yafham/fahima*
underwear ملابس داخلية *malaabis daakhiliyya*
undress خلع *khla`a*
unemployed عاطل عن العمل *`aatil `an al-`amal*
uneven متعرج/غير مستوي *muta`arrij/ghayr mustwaii*
universal عالمي *`aalamiy*
universality عالمية *`aalamiyah*
universe الكون *al kawn*
university جامعة *jaami`a*
unleaded بدون رصاص *biduun rasaas*
up على (فوق) *`alaa (fawq)*
upright منتصب *muntasib*
urge حث/يحث *hath-tha/yahuthu*
urgent ملح (عاجل) *mulih (`aajil)*
urgently بإلحاح (عاجلاً) *bi'ilhah (`aajilan)*
urine بول *bawl*
usual عادي *`aadii*
usually عادة *`aadatan*

V
vacate ترك/يترك *taraka/yatruk*
vacate أخلى/يخلي *akhlaa/yukhlii*
vacation عطلة (إجازة) *`utla (ijaaza)*
vaccinate لقح/يلقح *laq-qaha/yulaqqih*
vaccination تلقيح *talqiih*
vaccine لقاح *luqaah*
vagina المهبل *al-mahbal*
vain (in) عبثاً *`abathan*
valid قانوني/صالح *qaanuunii/saalih*
validate تصديق *tasdiiq*
validation مصادقة *musaadaqah*
valley وادي *waadii*
valuable ثمين *thamiin*
valuables أشياء ثمينة *ashyaa' thamiina*
value قيمة *qiimah*
values قيم *qiyam*

van عربة *`araba*
vase مزهرية *mazhariyya*
vegetable خضروات/خضار *khudrawaat/khudaar*
vegetarian نباتي *nabaatii*
vein وريد/عرق *wariid/`irq*
velvet مخمل *makhmal*
vending machine آلة بيع *aalat bay`*
venerate تبجيل *tabjiil*
venereal disease مرض تناسلي/ الزهرية *marad tanaasulii/ azzahriya*
venomous سام *saam*
vertical عمودي *`amuudii*
vertically عمودياً *`amuudiyan*
via عبر *`abra*
video camera كاميرا فيديو *kamiirat fiidiu*
view منظر *manzar*
village قرية *qarya*
virus فيروس *fairoos*
visa تأشيرة (فيزا) *ta'shiira (fizaa)*
vision رؤية *ru'yah*
visit (v.) زار/يزور *zaaraa/yazuur*
visit زيارة *ziyaara*
visiting time وقت الزيارة *waqt az-ziyaara*
visual بصري *basariy*
visualization تصور *tasawur*
visualize (v.) تصور/يتصور *tasawwara/yatasawwar*
vitamin tablets حبوب فيتامينات *hubuub vitaamiinaat*
vitamins فيتامينات *vitaamiinaat*
volcano بركان *burkaan*
volleyball كرة الطائرة *kuratu at-taa'irah*
vomit (v.) تقيأ *taqayya'*
vomit قيء/غثيان *qay'/ ghathayaan*

W

wait انتظر *intazara*
waiter نادل مطعم *naadil mat`am*
waiting room غرفة الانتظار *ghurfat al-intizaar*
waitress نادلة مطعم *naadilatu mat`am*
wake up نهض *nahada*
Wales ويلز *wiilz*
walk (n.) مشي*mashiy*
walk (v.) مشى *mashaa*
walking stick عكاز *`uk-kaaz*
wall حائط/جدار *haa'it/jidaar*
wallet محفظة نقود *mihfazat nuquud*
war حرب *harb*
wardrobe خزانة ثياب *khizaanat thiyaab*
warm دافئ *daafi'*
warn حذر/يحذر *hadh-dhara/ yuhadh-dhir*
warning تحذير *tahdhiir*
wash يغسل *yaghsil*
washing *ghasiil*
washing line حبل الغسيل *habl al-ghasiil*
washing machine غسالة/ماكينة غسيل *ghassala/maakinat ghasiil*
wasp دبور *dabbuur*

watch (v.) شاهد/يشاهد *shaahada/yushaahid*
watch ساعة *saa`ah*
water ماء *maa'*
waterfall شلال *shallaal*
waterproof مقاوم للماء *muqaawim lil maa'*
water-skiing تزلج على الماء *tazalluj `alaa al-maa'*
watery مائي *maa'iy*
way (direction) طريق *tariiq*
way (method) طريقة *tariiqah*
ways طرق *turuq*
we نحن *nahnu*
weak ضعيف *da`iif*
weakness ضعف *du`f*
wear لبس/يلبس *labisa/yalbas*
weather الطقس/الجو *at-taqs/al-jaw*
weather forecast الحالة الجوية *al-haala al-jawwiyya*
web موقع *mawqi`*
web browser محرك بحث *muharrik bahth*
webcam كاميرا ويب *kamira web*
webpage صفحة الموقع *safahat al mawqi`*
wed تزوج *tazaw-wuj*
wedding حفل زواج *haflu zawaaj*
Wednesday (يوم) الأربعاء *(yawm) arbi`aa'*
week أسبوع *usbuu`*
weekday يوم الأسبوع/يوم دوام *yawm dawaam/yawm alusbuu`*
weekdays أيام الأسبوع *ayyaam alusbuu`*
weekend عطلة نهاية الأسبوع *`utlat nihaayat al-usbuu`*
weekly أسبوعياً *usbuu`iyan*
weeks أسابيع *asaabi`*
weigh وزن/يزن *wazana/yazin*
weigh-out يزن *yazin*
weights أوزان *awzaan*
welcome أهلاً وسهلاً/مرحباً *marhaban/ahlan wa sahlan*
well (for water) بئر *bi'r*
well (good) جيد *jayyid*
west شرق *sharq*
wet رطب/مبلل *ratb/muballal*
wetsuit معطف مطري *mi`taf matarii*
What? ماذا؟ *Maadhaa?*
wheel عجلة *`ajala*
wheelchair كرسي مدولب/متحركة *kursii mudawlab/mutaharrik*
When? متى؟ *Mataa?*
Where? أين؟ *Ayna?*
Which? أي؟ *Ayy?*
white أبيض *abyad*
Who من *man*
Why? لماذا؟ *Limaadhaa?*
wide-angle lens عدسات متسعة الزوايا *`adasaat muttasi`at az-zawaaya*
widow أرملة *armala*
widower أرمل *armal*
wife زوجة *zawjah*
wind ريح *riih*
window (in room) شباك/نافذة *shubbaak/naafidha*
window (to pay) شباك الدفع *shubbaak ad-dafi`*